The Big Green Poetry Machine

Southern England

Edited by Claire Tupholme

First published in Great Britain in 2009 by:

Young Writers

Young Writers
Remus House
Coltsfoot Drive
Peterborough
PE2 9JX
Telephone: 01733 890066
Website: www.youngwriters.co.uk
All Rights Reserved
Book Design by Spencer Hart & Tim Christian
© Copyright Contributors 2008
SB ISBN 978-1-84431-967-1

Foreword

Young Writers' Big Green Poetry Machine is a showcase for our nation's most brilliant young poets to share their thoughts, hopes and fears for the planet they call home.

Young Writers was established in 1991 to nurture creativity in our children and young adults, to give them an interest in poetry and an outlet to express themselves. Seeing their work in print will encourage them to keep writing as they grow, and become our poets of tomorrow.

Selecting the poems has been challenging and immensely rewarding. The effort and imagination invested by these young writers makes their poems a pleasure to enjoy reading time and time again.

Contents

Bishop Tufnell CE Junior School, Bognor Regis 1
Julia McGee-Russell (11) 1
Georgia Kim Stevens (10) 1
Alexis Ellena Carey (10) 2
Bethany Jane Moignard (11) 2
Liberty Clegg (9) 3
Jessie Moon (10) 3
Charlotte Williamson (10) 4
Jessica Dawling (10) 4

Bisley Bluecoat School, Stroud 5
Laurie McCroddan (10) 5

Brook Field School, Swindon 5
Zoe Knight (9) 5
Anisha Kiran (8) 5
Ethan Corfield (8) 6
Joel Langley (8) 6
Elliott Bishop (8) 6
Ben Shepherd (8) 6
Leah Theobald (8) 7
Anica Yousaf (8) 7
Thomas Lawrence (8) 7
Pavneet Kaur Chahal (8) 7
Alecia Kissell (11) 8
Amy Sears (8) 8
Joshua Bowden (8) 8
Natasha Roy (10) 9
Lisa Smith (10) 9
Georgia Cotton (10) 10
Luke Jones (8) 10
Shanaye Thompson (8) 10
Katie Densham (10) 11
Nial Wright (8) 11
Emma Clayton (10) 12
Isabelle Sanderson (8) 12
Oliver Corfield (8) 12
Christopher-Paul Underhill (10) ... 13
Courtenay Williams (8) 13
Rebecca Jennings (8) 13
Lydia Clayton (10) 14
Evie Lawrence (8) 14
Alexandra Tong (10) 15
Megan Daw (10) 15
Charlotte Butler (11) 16
Haydn Witchell (10) 16
Loren James (10) 17
Harry Clayton (10) 17
Nikita Lucy Robinson (11) 18
Oliver Poulter (10) 18
Scarlet Leggett (10) 19
Ben Wright (10) 19
Ryan Kissell (11) 20

Cliffdale Primary School, Portsmouth 21
Violet Class (9) 21

Corpus Christi RC Primary School, Portsmouth 21
Daniel Maclaren (9) 21
Lewis Kyle (9) 21
Ellen McGill (9) 22
Joel Mathews (9) 22
Kassandra Underwood (9) 23
Marley Allen (9) 23
Owen Wood (9) 24
Kyle Phillips (10) 24
Chantal Hughes (8) 24
Emily Hume (9) 25
Aidan Leneghan (9) 25
Shannon McAndrew (9) 25
Dyan Marinda (8) 26
Thomas Ireton (9) 26
Samantha Rimmer (7) 26
Charis Almond (8) 27
Lauren Sedgewick (8) 27

Crowmarsh Gifford Primary School, Wallingford 27
James Nathan Willcox (8) 27
Charles Luck (9) 28
Joel Booker (8) 28
Max Prior (8) 29
Alex Winch (8) 29
Oliver Bird (9) 30
Christopher Teague (8) 30
Julie Quinn (8) 31
Helen (9) 31
Bella Kennedy (9) 32
Harry Mitson (9) 32
Beth Wilson (9) 32
Georgia Hewitt (9) 33

Matthew David Ferrett (8) 33
Liberty Spencer-Cosford (8) 34
Alexandra Miriam Payne (8) 34
Georgia Bray (8) 35
Harry Brown (9) 35
Joseph Payne (10) 36
Josie Arnold (9) 36
Lizzie Secker (9) 37
Matthew Alex Aplin (9) 37
Tabitha Gammer (9) 38
Ben Carrington (9) 38
Kate Tremayne (9) 39
Charlie Hodge (8) 39

Fairfields Primary School, Basingstoke 40
Georgia Tomkins (10) 40
Ashleigh Msipo (10) 40
Courtney Wallace (10) 40
Grace Blakeley (11) 41
Liam Stockdale (10) 41
Samantha Kimberley (11) 42
Luke Addo (10) 42
Thomas Hitching (11) 43
Louis Taylor (10) 43
Charlotte Kreiner (11) 44
Danny Sinclair (10) 44
Amber Stretton (10) 45
Alex Mosdell (11) 45
Anthony Burford (10) 46
Rachael Parker (10) 46
Joe Lloyd (10) 47
Lucas Freer (10) 47
Ellie Fraser (10) 48
Jasmine Flowerdew (10) 48
Alex Austen (10) 48
Iona De Chalons (10) 49
Nicholas Roche (11) 49
Dylan Bardell (10) 50
Ryan Turner (11) 50
Cardhelle Galapon (11) 51
Patience Miller (10) 51
Paul May-Miller (10) 51
Kerrie Buchanan (10) 52
Antony Crosby (10) 52
William Sully (10) 52
Luke Watts (10) 53
Allen Timbol (10) 53
Caitlin Cole (10) 54
Danny Schofield (10) 55

Maddie Vallis (10) 55
Lewis Frewer (10) 56
Samantha Pollock (10) 56
Luke Bowers (10) 56

Heathfield Junior School, Southampton 57
Rebecca Quinn (7) 57
Sapphire Lewis (7) 57
Rhonwen Ellis (7) 58
Ellie-Mae Lacey 58
Chloe Wilson (7) 58
Cari Ashman (8) 59
Chloe Wilkes 59
Rhianna Saunders (7) 59
Elli Woodhouse (7) 60
Charlie Rattley (7) 60

Holy Family Primary School, Bristol 60
Eden Byrne-Young (11) 60
Bethany Daniels (10) 61
Joseph Coutts Wood (10) 61
Matthew Watkins (11) 62
Hannah Pring (10) 62
Ella Wyatt (10) 62
Elena Bull (10) 63
William Duncan-Gibson (10) 63
Jack Scriven (10) 63
Sydney Fielden-Stewart (10) 64
Lydia Gillard (10) 64
Ben Green (10) 65
Nicole Walsh (11) 65
Jennifer Ashley 66

John Hampden Primary School, Thame 66
William Kendall (9) 66
Aysha Saeed (9) 67
James Reilly (9) 67

John Keble Memorial Primary School, Winchester 68
Eleanor Dickson (10) 68
Polly Pyke (10) 68
Sophie Patterson (11) 69

Millbrook Primary School, Grove 69
Georgina Ottley (8) 69
Sophie May Hadler (8) 70

Jordan Barker (8) 70
Matthew Moran (8) 71
Cameron Faulkner (8) 72
Josh King (8) 72
Elen Adshead (8) 73
Findlay Kerr (8) 73
Harry Bowman (8) 74
Joe Herbert (8) 75
Mollie Rose Davies (8) 76
Jodie Mathewson (8) 77
Joshua Othen (9) 77
Bonny Gao (8) 78
Jasmine Collins (8) 78
Tara Bevan (8) 79
Tiana Brady (8) 80
Jessica Clark (9) 81
Katie Sheath (9) 82
Lucy Titmuss (8) 83
Jack Cheshire (8) 84
Harriet Talbot (8) 85
Samuel Hinder (8) 86
Lee Stone (8) 87
Bethany Cassettari (8) 88
Ben Peirce Challenger (8) 88
Matthew Druce (8) 89
Robyn Thomas (8) 90
Hasan Bahar (9) 91
Joe Horton (9) 92
Lauren Hannah Goodenough (8) 93
Kurtis Conor Collins (8) 94
Olivia Simpson (8) 95
Harry Roberts (8) 95
Jessica Reeder (8) 96
Chloe Kilpin (8) 97
Georgina Dawson (8) 98

Oakwood Preparatory School, Chichester 98
Hannah Emerson (7) 98
Archie Lyndhurst (7) 99
Thea Morgan (7) 99
Noah Chisham (7) 99
Polly Williams (8) 100
Emily Bradford & Ella Johnson (7) 100
Felicity Davis (8) 101
Abigail Hoskins (7) 101
Amelia Pope (7) 102
Isabel Ebert & Kitty Williams (7) 102
Katie Wild (8) 103
Johnny Pardey & Hector Small (7) 103

Georgina Yeomans (9) 104
Bertille Michel & Ellie McDonald (7) 104
Emily Rose (9) 105
Fergus Bonar (8) 105
Luke Haddow (8) 106
Oscar Hughes (8) 106
Georgia McKirgan (9) 107
Eloise Flippance (10) 107
Max Rawlins (8) 108
Emma Russell (8) 108
Arabella Barwick (10) 109
Edward Williams (9) 109
Jack Congdon (10) 110
Mattie Hutchings (9) 110
Patrick Langmead (9) 111
Francesca Coulson (8) 111
Luke Connell (10) 112
Zoe Barnett (9) 112
Jasper Jellett (9) 113
Jaime Pardy (9) 114
Lloyd Morgan (9) 115
Ella Small (9) 115
Alexander McKirgan (10) 116
Bethany Williams (10) 116
Jake Goosen (10) 117
Katie Twist (10) 117
Ben Taylor (10) 118
James Webber (9) 118
Georgie Carter (10) 119
Elliot Ebert (10) 119
Laurie Emerson (10) 120
Jonathan Furniss & Philippa Noble (8) ..120
Fred Thomas (10) 120
Bobby Filary (10) 121
Bronte Popplewell (10) 122
David Brimecome (10) 122

St Alban's CE Primary School, Havant 123
Amy Frost (11) 123
Emily Frost (9) 123
Daisy Wiggins (9) 124
Daniel Aspey (10) 124
Georgina Mellor (10) 125
Johanna Horsman (10) 125
Joseph Walsh (11) 126
Samuel Horsman (8) 126
Nicholas Robertson (10) 127
Claudia Rowthorn (8) 127
Amy Shepherd (10) 128

Francesca Chalk (9) 128
Catherine Williams (8) 129
Andrew Briggs (7) 129
Harrison Blake Martin (7) 130
Julia Martin (7) 130
Isaac Morgan (8) 131
Toby Bunting (7) 131
Alice Kaminski (10) 132
Matthew Johnstone (7) 132
Matthew Lee (10) 133
Alfie Simms (9) 133
Bronwyn Flower-Bond (11) 134
Katherine Shepherd (7) 134
Madeleine Spice (10) 135
Mollie Griffiths (10) 135
Imogen Walsh (9) 136
Olivia Letchford (7) 136
Chloe Anderson (9) 136
Archie McKeown (8) 137
Euan Bonnar (8) 137

St John's Priory School, Banbury ... 138
Joseph Owen (8) 138
Lucy Shields (8) 138
Joshua Kearns (8) 139
Sean Daniels (8) 139
Thomas McGonagle (8) 139
Dylan Patel (8) 140
Meera Mahesh (8) 140
Stephen Marsden (8) 140
Harris MacPherson (8) 141
Emilia Fletcher (8) 141
Taya Eames (9) 141
Emma Robinson (8) 142

St Lawrence CE Primary School, Lechlade 142
Alex Hoad (10) 142

Sibford Junior School, Banbury 143
Sam Plank (9) 143
Amelia Proud (10) 143
Joseph Roxburgh (9) 144
George Woolley (9) 144
Darcey Mae Rivers (9) 145
Sidney Ocanigil-Tunstall (10) 145
Jack Brooks (7) 146
Ben Taylor (9) 146
Henry Jackson-Wells (7) 147
Hannah Gardiner (9) 147
Orla Gay (10) 147

Thomas Banbury (9) 148
Michael Rae (7) 148
Beth Hughes (10) 148
Parris Pratley (9) 149
Holly Martin (10) 149
Joseph Raybould (7) 150
Hayley Holland (10) 150

The Poems

The World Around Me

Winds whispering, my ragged clothes whipping around me.
Nowhere to turn.
Leaves crunching, frost biting, challenging all that stand in the way.
Nowhere to go.
Fire burning in a hearth that is not my own.
Nobody cares.
People laughing. Evil laughs. Poke me; prod me, till I'm bruised.
Riding through the dust and dirt.
Leaving me behind.
Silent snow, death is falling.
And I shiver, a Popsicle of ice.
Then my mother, who had been dead for years,
Lifting me up to a warmer place, a happier place,
Smiling and laughing all the way.
People walked by my body but it did not matter, for I was not there anymore.
Though I was in my body no longer, I still had my spirit.
For I am no longer homeless.

Julia McGee-Russell (11)
Bishop Tufnell CE Junior School, Bognor Regis

There's No Place Like Home

I have no home,
No snugly bed or warm thick sheets.
Just a cold wet pavement and a drenched cardboard box.

My clothes are thin and ripped and my shoes are torn and battered,
As the rain falls down: the cold freezing wind pierces through
my once warm heart.

I see people with love and families and I just wish I hadn't given that up because - now I have no home.

Georgia Kim Stevens (10)
Bishop Tufnell CE Junior School, Bognor Regis

Recycle Rap

Litter is dirty, litter is bad,
Throwing away rubbish makes us mad.
Our landfill sites are filling up,
So recycle all your plastic cups.
To recycle things you don't need, just pop
Along to your local charity shop.
It really helps our lovely earth,
To recycle things that have some worth.
The news we're trying to spread around,
Is don't drop litter on the ground.
It's really easy to reduce and reuse,
So help us tell others the great news.
Paper, clothes, tin cans and wood,
Can all be recycled and it's really good.

Alexis Ellena Carey (10)
Bishop Tufnell CE Junior School, Bognor Regis

Bad Streets

Cold, wet lonely that is what it is like on the streets,
The mossy, soggy grass fills your shoes.
Cold, wet, lonely, the littered streets feel dark
And as days go by the alleyways seem familiar
And being homeless is like having a storm following you.
Cold, wet, lonely, begging
As people go by they look in disgust
And shout foul language.
I know I will be on the streets until I die.
I'm scared, very scared, I don't want that day to come.
Do you want children on the streets?
If you don't, then do something about it!

Bethany Jane Moignard (11)
Bishop Tufnell CE Junior School, Bognor Regis

Being Homeless

Sitting there on the damp, dusty ground
People walking past, not even glancing in my direction
Why did it have to be me?
All alone, no one to comfort me
My father died in the war.
So why did it have to be me?
I've been homeless for as long as I remember,
My mother died when I was very young.
But why did it have to be me?
I now know but all hope is gone.
Just why did it have to be me?

Liberty Clegg (9)
Bishop Tufnell CE Junior School, Bognor Regis

Alone In The Big Wide World

Alone in the big wide world with no one to talk to
With no one to play with.
Just abandoned on the streets.
No family! I am lonely.
No friends! I am bored.
No food! I am starving.
No water! I am thirsty.
No shelter! I am cold
Help!
Please help me!
I know how those people on the street feel
Because I am one of them.

Jessie Moon (10)
Bishop Tufnell CE Junior School, Bognor Regis

Pollution And Global Warming

Pollution is . . .
Smoky air like the greyness of a dying flower,
Pollution is changing the colourful world into a bleak planet.
We are producing gas and we are killing our plants and living things.
Turn off the engine of your car,
That way we can start to save our poor planet and start afresh.

Global warming is . . .
The death of our planet, a hot fiery wrath that burns us miles from the sun.
It is wrecking the thin veil of the ozone layer,
We are producing lots of pollution that's burning the ozone layer
And could eventually kill our Earth.
Turn off your TVs and electricals now
Now we can save the world, together we can make a difference.

Charlotte Williamson (10)
Bishop Tufnell CE Junior School, Bognor Regis

Where Do We Go Now?

Where do we go now?
The trees are gone, the clouds are out,
The sun is hurting my eyes,
I come back from my hibernation and what a surprise.
Where do we go now?
My friends are gone, my family is gone
There is not much left.
I don't want it all to go,
So help me and save the rest.
Where do we go now?
No trees to climb, no air to breathe,
I can't move any further,
Up, up, up I go, you killed me you monsters.

Jessica Dawling (10)
Bishop Tufnell CE Junior School, Bognor Regis

Be Green Not Mean

Trees give us oxygen,
Cars give us pollution,
Switch to energy-saving bulbs,
That is my solution.

Turn off your taps,
Recycle dog food cans,
Give your clothes to charity,
Before the world goes down the pan.

Make a stand to woodcutters,
Before they chop trees down.
Recycle all your paper,
Keep the world green, safe and sound.

Laurie McCroddan (10)
Bisley Bluecoat School, Stroud

Recycling

Use both sides of paper,
Don't leave recycling till later,
Turn off taps when not in use,
Never litter, no excuse.

Zoe Knight (9)
Brook Field School, Swindon

Animals And Extinction

Don't lay traps, it could hurt,
Try to be friendly to the animals.
Do, do, do, do not hurt them
Every day the animals are dying.

Anisha Kiran (8)
Brook Field School, Swindon

Rainforest

There go the trees,
There go the animals
Chop, chop, chop,
One by one
Why can't they stop
And think about the environment?

Ethan Corfield (8)
Brook Field School, Swindon

Extinction Of Animals

Think about the animals that were all around us.
We don't see many of them because they're dying.
So look after the planet and help us out.
To stop the animals from getting killed.

Joel Langley (8)
Brook Field School, Swindon

The Animals End

The fantastic animals are running around
But men do not know what they're doing to them.
The moment the animals are coming to the end of their lives.

Elliott Bishop (8)
Brook Field School, Swindon

Recycling

Reduce, reuse and recycle to save our Planet Earth,
Pick up rubbish and recycle it.
Turn off taps and save water to help.
Switch off lights to save energy and electricity.

Ben Shepherd (8)
Brook Field School, Swindon

Animals And Extinction

All those animals in danger,
Frightened all day and night,
Please don't kill those animals,
Because we need to save our planet.

Leah Theobald (8)
Brook Field School, Swindon

Pollution

We should use our bikes more often
Because by using cars and motorbikes
It is making gas in the lovely sweet air
And everybody is breathing it in.

Anica Yousaf (8)
Brook Field School, Swindon

Litter

We should all do the same,
Pick up rubbish
And put it in a recycling bin,
Reduce, reuse, recycle.

Thomas Lawrence (8)
Brook Field School, Swindon

Help The Poor Animals

Help the poor animals
Lots of wonderful animals have been drowned.
A little polar bear is stuck in the middle of the ocean.
You have to help us.

Pavneet Kaur Chahal (8)
Brook Field School, Swindon

It's Easy

Anyone can recycle, it's easy!
Paper, cans, glass and plastic
Come on, don't be lazy,
The money we save is fantastic.

Come on, it's easy, anyone can recycle
Paper, cans, glass and plastic
Instead of your car, use your bicycle
We're saving the Earth that's fantastic.

Alecia Kissell (11)
Brook Field School, Swindon

Animals Extinction

Don't cause global warming
It doesn't save the ice world
Polar bears will become extinct
Just don't cause global warming today,
It upsets the world around us.

Amy Sears (8)
Brook Field School, Swindon

Pollution

Stop using cars,
Do more walking,
Save electricity,
Gas is killing animals,
The sea is destroyed.
Please save the Earth!

Joshua Bowden (8)
Brook Field School, Swindon

Earth

Have you ever thought about saving our planet?
Do you turn off the lights - when you aren't in the room?
Do you put on a jumper and turn down the heating?
Do you switch off the TV when you are not watching it?
Do you turn off the tap when you clean your teeth?
Do you walk or cycle rather than take the car?
Do you take the bus for long journeys?
Is your loft insulated at home? Why not, it saves energy.
We have all heard about recycling,
But do we recycle everything we can?
Bottles, paper and tin cans are just the tip of the iceberg
Why don't we build more wind turbines?
They might not look all that pretty but without them we might
                                      not have anything to look at.
Global warming damages our environment and animals could die.
If we carry on the way we are, we will not have any icebergs.

Natasha Roy (10)
Brook Field School, Swindon

Protect Our Future

The earth is our home, we should leave it alone,
Not clog it all up with cigarette butts.
It's a simple thing to do, to clean up after you.
Take home your litter, let's not get all bitter.
Don't create more pollution, let's work on a solution.

Stop cutting down our trees, how else will we breathe?
Our ice caps will disappear, polar bears won't be here.
The sea levels will rise, this should be no surprise.
Let's sort out this state, before it's too late.

Lisa Smith (10)
Brook Field School, Swindon

Everybody Can Be Green

To help the environment we all have to be green
And make our world look nice and clean.

When we write on paper, use each side,
Use your bike, not your car when you go for a ride.

Recycle your tins, bottles and cans,
Give them to the men that drive the recycling vans.

We can all be Eco-kids and keep the world green
But not without the help of the big green poetry machine.

Georgia Cotton (10)
Brook Field School, Swindon

The Way To Not Litter

When I walk around
I can see litter on the ground
So everyone now needs to
Reduce, reuse and recycle
To help our Eco-world.

Luke Jones (8)
Brook Field School, Swindon

Wonderful Animals

Little wonderful animals,
Lots of wonderful animals are dying.
We should try to help them,
Because they are getting killed by horrid people
Who want lots of money.

Shanaye Thompson (8)
Brook Field School, Swindon

Not Just Me

What can I do, I'm only small
There's only one of me
I could say nothing
And watch it all on TV
I could leave it to other people
To try to save the world
But no!
I can use both sides of the paper
Or pick up litter and not walk on by
I can recycle cans
I can reduce the things I buy
I can walk to school
And tell my mum not to drive.
I can reuse plastic bottles that I drink
I cannot waste the food I eat
But that's just me.
Together we
Could stop producing pollution
Stop over-fishing the seas
Cure incurable disease
And not cut down the trees
But most of all we could save our planet
By working as a team.

Katie Densham (10)
Brook Field School, Swindon

Pollution

Stop using cars
Always walk
Save electricity and
Stop to pick up litter!

Nial Wright (8)
Brook Field School, Swindon

The Green Machine

T hink green, the planet is in your hands,
H ave you made your eco-plans?
E nergy is fading like waves crushing the sands.

G reen is the world of today,
R educe, reuse and recycle in every way,
E ven May will be cold if you don't do as you're told,
E very day rainforests die,
N ever litter otherwise the climate will sigh.

M ake Mother Nature happy,
A nd you be a good chappy,
C hange the climate, help the primates, be snappy,
H elp the homeless, get a bonus, they'll be happy,
I f the war does not stop, it will destroy us all,
N ever throw the chance to stand and call
E veryone does it today.

Emma Clayton (10)
Brook Field School, Swindon

Wildlife In Danger

Animals are dying from the diseases of the Earth
Our environment is in danger.
The workers don't care
So stop killing animals, stop, stop, stop!

Isabelle Sanderson (8)
Brook Field School, Swindon

Litter

Do pick up litter
And put it in a bin
To save the planet.

Oliver Corfield (8)
Brook Field School, Swindon

Human Awareness

Poverty is bad,
Africa is full of it,
Help the people now.

Rainforests cut down
There is no air to breathe now
All the trees have gone.

Christopher-Paul Underhill (10)
Brook Field School, Swindon

Animals Die

The animals are dying
The Earth is crying
As more and more animals die in traps.
Or maybe from chemicals from testers
Or poison in the sea or on land.
I can hear wailing from the world above.

Courtenay Williams (8)
Brook Field School, Swindon

Wonderful Animals

Lots of wonderful animals
Are getting destroyed.
They're jumping wild and free
Until they get stolen.
Now loads of animals have no homes.

Rebecca Jennings (8)
Brook Field School, Swindon

The Planet Is Changing

Run, run, run it's here.
Hide, hide, hide in fear.
The ozone layer is about to disappear.
If you don't save it,
You'll pay for it.
If you say why the grass is yellow?
Well fellow I know where you've gone wrong
Help the planet before it's gone.
But if you do as you please.
Beware of the disease.
I pity the people who litter.
Because the planet is dying quicker.
The rainforests are falling.
You are appalling wasting it away like that.
The animals are at extinction point.
What do you think to do?
The pollution is rising.
But that is not surprising.
Remember November that could be hot.
But there is a way to alter the plot.
Don't give up hope and be a dope.
There's something you can do.
Just reduce, reuse, and recycle.

Lydia Clayton (10)
Brook Field School, Swindon

Animals Are In Danger

The animals are dying
And the Earth is in danger of diseases
Like ice melting to water
Animals are dying, no, no, no!

Evie Lawrence (8)
Brook Field School, Swindon

Think!

Stop!
Think, somewhere out there is a family, homeless with no clean water.
Think, Mother Earth is being covered with a blanket of litter,
                                     growing every second.
Think, animals in all corners of the world suffering because of us.
Think, every time you drive to your local school or shop you help
                                     pollute our environment.
Is this really how we want to live?
Think, what would we lose if we gave a few pennies a week to
                                     those who need it?
Think, would it be too difficult to walk an extra couple of metres to
                                     put your waste in the bin?
Think, if we simply use both sides of the paper, we can help
                                     save the trees that millions of animals live in.
Think, would it be asking a lot to walk to places you can,
                                     instead of destroying the ozone layer.
Think, how could you make our world a better place?

Alexandra Tong (10)
Brook Field School, Swindon

Green And Care

  G ive care to what you throw away and what you recycle.
  R ethink how you travel, you could even walk or cycle.
  E levate the happiness, not the carbon dioxide.
  E very day fresh air inside and outside.
  N ow think what you can do.

Reduce, reuse, recycle
Then we will have a happy, healthy Earth.

Megan Daw (10)
Brook Field School, Swindon

Animals In Danger

Look around you, what can you see?
Is this the world you want it to be?

People don't understand
How we can share this peaceful land.
Animals have been found dead
Because poachers have shot them right through the head.
Extinction will come if their homes are lost.
Big companies succeed at a terrible cost.

Are you really mad
Or just extremely sad?
Well you can help by telling others
What they must do.
Helping the animals is really up to you.
Choose carefully and buy Fair Trade
The money goes straight to where it is made.

Look around you, what can you see?
Help save the animals,
Come and join me!

Charlotte Butler (11)
Brook Field School, Swindon

Colours

I'm not yellow
I'm not orange
I'm not pink
I'm not purple

I am green
I recycle.

Haydn Witchell (10)
Brook Field School, Swindon

Rainforests

I walk into the rainforest
What can I see?
A monkey swinging in a tree.

A little way in
What can I hear?
Squawking parrots, have no fear.

Deep inside
What can I smell?
Dampness surrounds me, slippery, I nearly fell.

Further still
What can I taste?
Gushing water, going to waste.

Why are we destroying this beautiful place?
Just to give us some more space
Animals' homes are getting lost
Do you want to pay this cost?

Loren James (10)
Brook Field School, Swindon

Recycle

R ecycle things you can.
E verybody join in and recycle.
C ans, paper, everything you can just recycle.
Y ell out, 'Recycle!'
C are for the environment, it is precious.
L isten to what I say.
E ncourage your friends and neighbours and help them to recycle.

Harry Clayton (10)
Brook Field School, Swindon

My Green Poem

We all share our planet
So don't be greedy,
Think of the needy.
Don't drive too fast
Make your gas last,
Don't be a fool
Save fuel to be cool.
A throwaway society
That's no good to us,
Reduce, reuse, recycle
That is a plus,
Don't be mean
And try to be green.
Litter and pollution
We need a solution.
So do what's right
And sort out our endangered species' plight.

Nikita Lucy Robinson (11)
Brook Field School, Swindon

The Greatest Enemy Is Us

Our world is choking
But isn't smoking,
Is pollution doing it in?
Recycling plastic
Isn't so drastic
Glass, paper and tin
Illness and diseases are increasing
But rainforests and trees are depleting
Is this what we want for our world?

Oliver Poulter (10)
Brook Field School, Swindon

Saving The Planet

Earth needs saving, it's easy to do
Anyone can help, so why don't you.
Reduce, reuse, recycle your plastic, glass and paper
Turn off the lights, don't be a waster.
The floor is not a bin; to drop litter is a sin
Pick it up and put it in,
Tell people around you to use the bin.
Trees are important, they keep the planet alive
If you cut down the rainforests, the Earth might die.
Plants give animals, their only food and shelter,
To take them away would be a big disaster.
Electric cars are green, they spread less pollution,
Share a car or walk, that may be the solution.
Help save the world and make it a better place!

Scarlet Leggett (10)
Brook Field School, Swindon

Save The Earth

We all need to do our thing
Putting things in recycling bins
Newspaper, cans, boxes and bags
It's so, so easy
Recycle your paper
Pick up your waste
Reduce, reuse, recycle
Save the Earth today.

Ben Wright (10)
Brook Field School, Swindon

Don't Dump The Rubbish

From plastic bottles,
To metal cans,
Recycle them,
Start making plans.

Don't dump the rubbish on the Earth,
Just remember what it's worth!
Recycle or reuse or compost things,
Apple cores, glass bottles or tree cuttings.

Don't forget, energy use:
Your lights and TV settings,
You need to reduce!

Not just us but the animals too,
We're ruining the temperatures for animals like in the zoo.
Polar bears on icebergs melting away,
Stranded at sea with nowhere to stay.

Don't dump the rubbish on the Earth,
Just remember what it's worth!
Recycle or reuse or compost things,
Apple cores, glass bottles or tree cuttings.

Sometimes you use things that you take for granted,
But next time when you do, remember and think:
Is it worth killing and destroying?
Just for pleasure, luxury or something.

Ryan Kissell (11)
Brook Field School, Swindon

Recycling - Do Your Bit!

R ecycling is the only way
U se your green bin every day.
B ottles and cans in the green bin
B ut kitchen waste for composting.
I n my school we're very clean
S orting rubbish, aren't we keen
H ave you done your bit?

Violet Class (9)
Cliffdale Primary School, Portsmouth

Octopoem

Recycling is emerald green
On a beaming hot summer's day
In a backyard
On a wonderful tropical day
A yellow T-shirt, which has orange spots on it
A large, comfy, blue flowered sofa
Characters from a fairy tale which means a happy ending
A red strawberry because it's healthy and it's good for you.
Recycle, it's good for the environment!

Daniel Maclaren (9)
Corpus Christi RC Primary School, Portsmouth

Recycling Today

Recycling today
We love to help our world
Do you care like me?

Lewis Kyle (9)
Corpus Christi RC Primary School, Portsmouth

Go Green

Plastic bags are pointless to us,
400 years but they are still not gone
Undisposable and a waste to us
What do we do?

Unless we do something now
It could affect our lives forever
Just sitting there in a rubbish heap
What do we do?

We must go green
It will be a happier life
A better future for all of us
We can do it!

Ellen McGill (9)
Corpus Christi RC Primary School, Portsmouth

Reuse

Keep the world healthy
Pollution is horrible
Save the world today

Help recycling
Bottles go to bottle banks
Save the planet now

Do your duty now
Use your recycling bin
Take care of our place.

Joel Mathews (9)
Corpus Christi RC Primary School, Portsmouth

Recycle

Reuse, reclaim and recover
No matter what you call it,
Our habitat is dying,
We must try to restore it.

Retrieve it, salvage it,
Save electricity,
Our planet really needs it,
I hope you all agree.

Don't drive to school,
Because it will increase your carbon footprint,
Turn off the tap and the lights
And recycle, recycle, recycle.

Kassandra Underwood (9)
Corpus Christi RC Primary School, Portsmouth

Recycle Busters

Everyone loves the bottle bank,
Like a great big tank,
But some people don't care about recycling,
Some people just throw rubbish on the floor,
Some people recycle things that you can't recycle,
Like . . .
Chocolate bars, sweet wrappers and more,
The things that you should recycle are
Plastic, tins, glass bottles and newspapers
So recycle now before it's too late.

Marley Allen (9)
Corpus Christi RC Primary School, Portsmouth

Untitled

Planting fruit and vegetables is growing green
On a dazzling summer's day
Planted in an open field
During an enjoyable, gleaming day
Growing vegetables in a messy top and trousers
Like a colourful flowery rug
They are farmers in a gardening show
Beautiful tomatoes, sprouts and pumpkins.

Owen Wood (9)
Corpus Christi RC Primary School, Portsmouth

Recycling

Recycling is what I do . . .
I eat bottles for breakfast
Paper for lunch
Cans for dinner
People give me stuff to crunch!
I give it back reprocessed, ready for reuse
Recycling is what I do . . .

Kyle Phillips (10)
Corpus Christi RC Primary School, Portsmouth

Go Green

G o green to help make a new spotless and clean world
O pen a valuable day and live peacefully

G ive a tremendous hug to a polished world
R elease and cleanse the loving world
E nd the dirty day
E very day you must clean
N ever forget to recycle.

Chantal Hughes (8)
Corpus Christi RC Primary School, Portsmouth

Octopoem

Carbon footprints are a cold damp coal of black
On a misty, foggy winter's night
Ambushed in a dusky prison cell
They are a polluting storm heading our way
Cramped, itchy, ripped rags
A destroyed, prickly, graffitied concrete
They are characters from a horror film
Rotten, decaying stale bread.

Emily Hume (9)
Corpus Christi RC Primary School, Portsmouth

Go Green Today

I am a light bulb,
Never getting to sleep,
Hoping to be turned off,
Hoping to be replaced
With a better one than me.
Energy efficient, now I'm better.

Aidan Leneghan (9)
Corpus Christi RC Primary School, Portsmouth

Octopoem

Carbon footprints are a hateful black
On a windy winter's night
Trapped in a horrid cell
They cause a terrible flood of oil
Uncomfortable itchy clothes
Draped in a graffiti place
Carbon footprints are a hateful black.

Shannon McAndrew (9)
Corpus Christi RC Primary School, Portsmouth

Recycle

R emember to recycle
E verybody should do their best
C lear our world
Y ou will recycle
C lear up the litter
L ittering is not good
E veryone, let's grab a green bin!

Dyan Marinda (8)
Corpus Christi RC Primary School, Portsmouth

Carbon Footprints

Carbon footprints are evil,
They are produced by car engines,
Smoke and pollution.
Carbon footprints are produced by everyone.
Grow plants and save the planet.
Reduce your carbon footprint.

Thomas Ireton (9)
Corpus Christi RC Primary School, Portsmouth

Go Green

G o and start to recycle
O n the street, in the park, anywhere

G o and use your green bin
R efresh the world
E veryone should start to go green
E very day you can recycle
N ever stop - go green.

Samantha Rimmer (7)
Corpus Christi RC Primary School, Portsmouth

Go Green

G et to work, recycle
O pen the door to a new world

G o on, try it yourself
R emember to help the planet
E verything matters
E ncourage your friends to help
N ow it's your turn!

Charis Almond (8)
Corpus Christi RC Primary School, Portsmouth

Untitled

We should recycle,
Never let our planet down,
Are you helping us?

Lauren Sedgewick (8)
Corpus Christi RC Primary School, Portsmouth

The World's End

I see trees chopped down.
I hear animals screaming.
I feel pollution.
I smell bad things.

Reduce, reuse and recycle.

I see flowers growing.
I hear birds singing.
I feel oxygen.
I smell a happy world.

James Nathan Willcox (8)
Crowmarsh Gifford Primary School, Wallingford

My Feeling Poem

I feel bad because the dump men
Are throwing away useable stuff.
I can hear fish screaming.
I can smell pollution!
I can see trash everywhere.

Reduce, reuse, recycle.

I see a wonderful wonderland.
I hear birds chirping.
I feel fresh green grass.
I smell fresh air.

Charles Luck (9)
Crowmarsh Gifford Primary School, Wallingford

Environment

I see pollution
I hear screams
I feel badness
I smell rubbish.

Reduce, reuse, recycle.

I see green
I hear the forest
I feel wind
I smell the flowers.

Joel Booker (8)
Crowmarsh Gifford Primary School, Wallingford

Pollution

I see cans, I see tins,
I hear animals getting caught in bins.
I feel sad for all the animals that are dying out there.
I smell pollution, I smell smoke.

Recycle, reduce, refuse, reuse.

I see countryside, I see growing trees,
I hear birds, I feel wind
And now I'm happy for all animals,
I smell grass, I smell trees.

Max Prior (8)
Crowmarsh Gifford Primary School, Wallingford

Environment

I see horrible countryside
I hear sounds of fire
I smell smelly litter
I feel really sad.

Reduce, reuse, recycle.

I see beautiful countryside
I hear the trees blowing
I smell lovely flowers
I feel really happy.

Alex Winch (8)
Crowmarsh Gifford Primary School, Wallingford

I See ...

I see tall piles of rubbish nearly everywhere I look,
I see oil floating in the rivers,
I see lots of smog,
I see dead fish lying on the riverbanks,
I see smoke rising into the clouds.

I smell smoke polluting the air and killing the birds,
I smell rubbish on the pavement,
I feel guilty for the world,
I feel angry with the people who leave rubbish on the floor,
I hear the rubbish blowing along the ground.

Recycle, reduce, reuse.
I see the flowers blowing along with the breeze,
I see the green grass on top of the hills,
I smell the buttercups swaying in the wind,
I feel happy with everyone who has tried to save the world,
I hear the birds singing in their nests.

Oliver Bird (9)
Crowmarsh Gifford Primary School, Wallingford

Environment Poem

I see manky rivers that have been polluted.
I hear cars and vehicles.
I feel sad and disappointed.
I smell rotten food and revolting smells.

Recycle, reduce, reuse.

I see fresh green grass.
I hear animals and nature.
I feel a fresh cool breeze.
I smell pollen from the flowers.

Christopher Teague (8)
Crowmarsh Gifford Primary School, Wallingford

It's All Our Fault

We dumped the rubbish on the floor.
We killed the animals in the sea,
It's not just you and me, it's all of us,
All of us, you see.
We don't recycle, we don't reuse,
But if we did I'm sure you'll see,
It's not just you and me
That dumps our rubbish on the floor
But if we did recycle
Maybe it would help the world go green.

Julie Quinn (8)
Crowmarsh Gifford Primary School, Wallingford

Senses

I see tins, paper bags and sharp bottle tops
At the seaside where they shouldn't be.
I hear birds squawking with fear
For their heads are stuck in a sharp metal bottle holder.
I feel angry, upset, guilty all at the same time.
I smell burning trees.

Recycle, reduce, reuse.

I see waves crashing over the clean sandy beach.
I hear birds singing in happiness.
I feel happy, green, relaxed.
I smell the flowers in the sunshine.

Helen (9)
Crowmarsh Gifford Primary School, Wallingford

Recycle

R ecycle all of your rubbish!
E verything is changing, everything is not the way it used to be.
C hange the world with a bin at your door,
Y es, we need your help.
C ome, you could save an animal's life,
L iving somewhere in a tree, may turn into the wood in your fire.
E ars that hear the sea may not know what is happening in it.
   I want to help the environment.

Bella Kennedy (9)
Crowmarsh Gifford Primary School, Wallingford

Environment

This stream is not a nice place, it is a big disgrace.
It is all dark and brown like a chocolate bar.
The plants are overgrowing, we need to do something.
Why did this happen? I really don't know.
I want to clear the river, cut the plants and let new ones grow.
I just want to go out there and save the *world*.

Harry Mitson (9)
Crowmarsh Gifford Primary School, Wallingford

Recycle

R euse your rubbish, you never know what you can do.
E ncourage your friends and family and show them
   what you have done.
C ycle or walk, don't get in the car.
Y ou can always go your bit to help the plants to grow.
C an you hear the cars go by causing pollution?
L earn what you can do to stop the animals dying.
E veryone can recycle, so do it!

Beth Wilson (9)
Crowmarsh Gifford Primary School, Wallingford

World Of Misery

Look around, what do you see?
Do you see a dull world of misery?
You will not see much, with a world full of dust.

You can hear a machine making dull clouds,
And you won't see all the beautiful views.
So I will give you some useful clues along the way!
Do you want to make this a non-litter place?
You would be killing wildlife and nature,
They've done nothing wrong have they?

These colours make you feel useless really
So let's change red, black, dark blue and grey,
Turn them into happy colours like light red, blue, green and yellow.
To help the world we could cut down on the electricity
And cycle to school instead of drive.
This could save our world!

Georgia Hewitt (9)
Crowmarsh Gifford Primary School, Wallingford

Helping The World Stay A Better Place

I see a world of rubbish bags in the trees,
Newspapers on the ground, green water in the lakes.
I hear lots of birds flying away because of all of the pollution in the air.
I smell lots of bad gas and pollution and lots of bad air.

Recycle, reduce, reuse.

I see lots of wonderful stuff like ducks in lakes.
I hear birds tweeting in the trees.
I feel the fresh green grass.

Matthew David Ferrett (8)
Crowmarsh Gifford Primary School, Wallingford

Pollution

I see the world dying by humans dropping rubbish.
I feel rubbish, rubbish, rubbish.
I hear screams of suffocating animals.
I smell pollution drifting everywhere.

Reduce, reuse, recycle.

I see flowers growing and birds nesting.
I feel the soft earth.
I hear the world again.
The world is a wonderful place.

Liberty Spencer-Cosford (8)
Crowmarsh Gifford Primary School, Wallingford

Help The Environment

I see lots of rubbish and junk.
I hear birds dying.
I feel dirt blowing around me.
I smell rivers which are really smelly.

Recycle, reduce, reuse.

I see the bright blue sky.
I hear fish splattering their tails.
I feel fresh wind.
I smell flowers.

Alexandra Miriam Payne (8)
Crowmarsh Gifford Primary School, Wallingford

Environment

I see the polluting which makes me feel sad
In all ways I hate it like this, with grey cloudy days.
I hear the coughing which makes me feel bad,
Sometimes I think it's up to my super mum and dad.

Recycle, reduce, reuse.

I see the flowers grow and children all know
That it is clean and we will stay here.
I hear trees rustling in the warm breeze.
I feel clear cold windows on my mum's car
And that's how I like it.

Georgia Bray (8)
Crowmarsh Gifford Primary School, Wallingford

The Jolly Green Bin

I am your recycling bin,
You can put paper, card and tin in.
I go on a journey in a recycling machine
I come out nice and clean.
We have to look after the world
We want to try to keep it turning
So we have to look after our world
And keep it clean and then the Earth will gleam.

Harry Brown (9)
Crowmarsh Gifford Primary School, Wallingford

Environment

E arth is a polluting planet
N ature is dying
V ehicles release carbon dioxide
I think we should do something
R educe, reuse and recycle
O ther people help to save the planet
N eed to recycle
M ake new power
E lectric needs saving
N o polluting the planet
T hank you for saving the Earth.

Joseph Payne (10)
Crowmarsh Gifford Primary School, Wallingford

Environment

E very day, the world gets polluted
N o beaches have deep blue sea anymore
V ery grey skies are starting to emerge
I n China, London and many more cities
R ain clouds appear in many strange places
O nly we can save the Earth
N ow all the ice in the Arctic is melting
M any animals are becoming extinct
E veryone could do little things to help
N ot leaving on lights, walking to school
T hen the world would be a better place.

Josie Arnold (9)
Crowmarsh Gifford Primary School, Wallingford

Pick Up Litter!

P ick up litter,
I don't want to be a sitter,
C an you stop endangered animals dying?
K ick up your system, come on let's start trying?

U p, down, litter everywhere,
P ollution is bad, it makes people stare.

L ook around, what do you see?
I see a world of misery,
T ry to recycle and reuse and save the world,
T o clean the environment, boys and girls,
E nvironments will be happy and safe,
R ecycle, reduce, come on, let's have faith!

Lizzie Secker (9)
Crowmarsh Gifford Primary School, Wallingford

A Dead World

A dead world?

D riving around is killing the
E arth, war and bombs
A re doing harm to animals
D o we care? Will we care?

W e will do our bit and
O ur world will be clean
R educe, reuse and recycle
L et nature be
D econtamination!

Matthew Alex Aplin (9)
Crowmarsh Gifford Primary School, Wallingford

Don't Drop Litter!

Put your rubbish in the bin.
Safe from the ground and the creatures all around.
Pick up the litter other people drop.
If it's messy, get a mop.
Walk to school, it's so cool.
Don't go in the car, even if it's far.
Do you have a green bin?
Put things in there
Or make a cardboard house for your teddy bear.
Put your rubbish in the bin.
Safe from the ground
And the creatures all around.

Tabitha Gammer (9)
Crowmarsh Gifford Primary School, Wallingford

Help World

I am a robot
I weigh a tonne
I can read and write
I can do anything
The power station is killing everything
The Earth is dying
I can smell it
I can hear it roar
The flames rise high
I will stop this
Trash it down
Reduce, reuse, recycle
Reduce, reuse, recycle.

Ben Carrington (9)
Crowmarsh Gifford Primary School, Wallingford

Don't Litter!

D ay by day people litter,
O nly people don't care!
N obody really thinks,
T his world could be a lovely place.

L itter is bad,
I n some places animals are sad!
T oday we could make a difference.
T ry, come on, you know we can!
E verybody can make a difference so,
R eally try, this world could be beautiful!

Kate Tremayne (9)
Crowmarsh Gifford Primary School, Wallingford

Untitled

I see pollution.
I hear birds flapping in the tip.
I smell smoke.
I feel sick.

Reduce, reuse, recycle.

I see birds flying in the sky.
I smell fresh air.
I feel happy.

Charlie Hodge (8)
Crowmarsh Gifford Primary School, Wallingford

Recycle Your Rubbish

Many people ignore the fact that
they should recycle.
But whatever could be recycled,
People throw it away.
They either throw it in the wrong bin,
or on the streets.
Please help our environment
Be a safe, clean, tidy place to live.
Recycle your rubbish!

Georgia Tomkins (10)
Fairfields Primary School, Basingstoke

Rainforest

Being in a wildly beautiful rainforest is wonderful
But seeing a rainforest being destroyed is worse than I thought.
Do you know that people are cutting trees down in rainforests
And turning them into paper? *I was horrified.*
The Earth has got to change into a better place.
If people didn't cut all the trees you could have imagined
How this place would have looked.
All of the animals would have been happy
But you have endangered their habitat.

Ashleigh Msipo (10)
Fairfields Primary School, Basingstoke

Commotion In The Rainforest At Dawn

Trees stretching to the sky and the birds flying over hills
Water going over rocks getting wet.
Birds flying over hills with water going over the rocks
And getting wet and the birds sitting on the trees.

Courtney Wallace (10)
Fairfields Primary School, Basingstoke

Climate Change Is Happening

Whether you like it or not,
Climate change is happening rapidly
Coming from the polar ice caps
Thick cold chunks of shimmering ice
Melting
Water levels are rising
It's started
Danger
Uncontrollable flooding
Leaving many homeless
Danger
It has to stop
Now!

Grace Blakeley (11)
Fairfields Primary School, Basingstoke

Rainforests

Rainforests are always drizzly,
Because there are rainy clouds in the sky.
Also there are showers that plummet,
Some animals like it,
Others don't as the shower contains drops.
Trees and plants contain oxygen and chlorophyll,
And both have leaves.
The rainforest is peaceful and quiet
And has beautiful waterfalls;
Therefore heed this warning tree cutters,
Save the rainforests,
Don't cut down trees!

Liam Stockdale (10)
Fairfields Primary School, Basingstoke

The Mess Of The World

People live on me,
I am their life.
My mystical waters reflect the good of me.
But then . . .
Bang!
Chop!
Trees are gone.
How will you breathe?

Pow!
Kick!
Animals are gone.
Do you want extinction?

Choke!
Drive!
The world's heating up.
Do you want to be flooded?

You are killing me,
So I will kill you,
I fade,
Perish,
Die.

Samantha Kimberley (11)
Fairfields Primary School, Basingstoke

The Air

The air, the air, pull up a chair,
The air, no one cares,
Think about bears,
Think about trees
And think about oxygen
And families.

Luke Addo (10)
Fairfields Primary School, Basingstoke

Pollution

Lots of cars passing
You should start recycling.
Pollution!
Stop your graffiti
Don't drive your Audi TT
Ride your bike instead
And don't laze around
In your bed.
Save the world
Stop polluting.
Pollution!
Look at the world now
Start to feel proud
You've done something good.

Thomas Hitching (11)
Fairfields Primary School, Basingstoke

Pollution

I was watching TV one day.
I saw the news.
The ice was melting quickly.
Dying and breaking.
North and South Pole.
It was very bold.
We were polluting the world.
Lots to do.
People now had a clue.
We have to work hard
And stop polluting the world!

Louis Taylor (10)
Fairfields Primary School, Basingstoke

Pollution

It's in the air
It's in the sea
It's there right in front of me
It cuts down trees
And fills the holes
It kills the cows
It kills the sheep
And poisons the milk that we drink
It's in the cars
And comes through the exhaust
Gets in the lungs and they are no more
It's in the ground and around the Earth
If we don't do something soon, we will surely burst.

Charlotte Kreiner (11)
Fairfields Primary School, Basingstoke

War

Menacing planes fly overhead,
Dropping dangerous cargo,
Deadly guns firing bullets,
Lightning speed,
Dangerous war, men fighting each other,
Boats floating on the sea,
Shooting their big guns,
Why can't the war stop?

Danny Sinclair (10)
Fairfields Primary School, Basingstoke

Please, Please Give Me A Home

I am so cold,
Give me a home.
Give me something to eat,
I am very hungry.
I am very ill and sad,
Please, please give me a home.
Give me some medicine
And something to hug.
I need a drink,
Please, please give me a home.
I have a sore throat,
Please, please give me a home.

Amber Stretton (10)
Fairfields Primary School, Basingstoke

Rainforest

A rainforest is a quiet untroubled place.
Well it was.
Until people began to cut it down for their own needs.
We must protect the rainforests
Before they all die out.
We need to plant more trees.
We need to use less paper.
A rainforest is home to lots of animals
And if the rainforest goes, so do the animals.

Alex Mosdell (11)
Fairfields Primary School, Basingstoke

My Pollution Poem

I looked closely
At the nuclear,
Smoking factory pipes.
What a complete mess!
The carbon dioxide
Absorbing precious oxygen
That we need
So think slowly
Before you get in your car!
Or maybe
You should cycle more
Walk or cause more traffic
It's your choice so make it quick.

Anthony Burford (10)
Fairfields Primary School, Basingstoke

Litter

Litter, the world's killer
There are crisp packets, polystyrene packs
There are fishing nets and cigarettes
Litter is lying around like a . . .
Musty
Muddy
Mucky
Mess.

Rachael Parker (10)
Fairfields Primary School, Basingstoke

Litter, Litter Everywhere

Lots of litter everywhere,
It makes me wonder,
Why people don't care.
Soon the world will be covered
By huge landfills of plastic bags.
Some things could have been recycled,
But no one thinks,
So next time you go shopping
Please think twice.
Bring your own bag.

Joe Lloyd (10)
Fairfields Primary School, Basingstoke

Litter On The Streets

I looked out of my window,
What a mess!
Mucky, malodorous litter
And miniature pieces of plastic
Pounded by masses of feet.
More and more litter
Dropped on the ground.
Claggy lolly sticks and rotting food
But the plastic will still be around
For years and years and years . . .
Why don't people think?

Lucas Freer (10)
Fairfields Primary School, Basingstoke

Homeless People

Homeless people are dirty and smelly.
Everything they own is carried in an old tatty bag.
They ask for food and money
Or search the rubbish bins.
Their clothes are scruffy and never get washed.
They sleep in doorways or under bridges.
Why do we let this happen?

Ellie Fraser (10)
Fairfields Primary School, Basingstoke

Rainforest

With the big bushy trees and all the fruit
The animals can live,
But if people keep coming,
To take it all
There'll be nothing left,
All the animals will die
And an overflowing waterfall
Their homes will get washed away.

Jasmine Flowerdew (10)
Fairfields Primary School, Basingstoke

Pollution

Do people only think of themselves?
Think before you throw anything away!
Beware pollution, think about the animals like penguins.
They might get plastic rings stuck around their necks.
We are making animals extinct.
Is this fair?

Alex Austen (10)
Fairfields Primary School, Basingstoke

Animals

Many people have pets
Like cute, cuddly rabbits,
Soft, furry kittens,
Colourful birds,
Golden, scaly fish,
Adorable, tiny hamsters,
But there are other animals,
Like small, homeless birds
From us cutting down trees,
Huge cats dying
From us killing for fur,
Ill sea creatures,
From pollution,
Wild rhinos and elephants killed for their ivory,
So let's all care for any animal big or small.

Iona De Chalons (10)
Fairfields Primary School, Basingstoke

Animals

Animals get extinct.
Hunted for food and warmth.
Living creatures alive then dead.
Don't hunt the animals.
Don't hunt the Earth.
Cooked one day, eaten the other.
Remember the animals.
Remember the Earth.
Keep the animals.

Nicholas Roche (11)
Fairfields Primary School, Basingstoke

Poverty

The people are very poor.
The people have no money.
They have nothing to eat but rotten apples.
They do nothing but beg.
Every time they see people go by it's promising for money.
But they don't give any not even 1p.
Please help these old, mucky people
Because they can't live like this.
They've got no clean water
And death is closer for them.
Closer.
Closer.
Closer.

Dylan Bardell (10)
Fairfields Primary School, Basingstoke

Save The Rainforest

Save the excellent, beautiful rainforest
Animals live there and you chop down their homes
There are only a few left!
Don't cut down the green trees
Recycle your paper
Cutting down trees is bad
If you chop down trees
Terrible carbon dioxide will stay
And no more oxygen will come . . .
You will die!

Ryan Turner (11)
Fairfields Primary School, Basingstoke

Pollution Problem

Pollution in the Earth is a nasty taste,
Now the world would be a smelly place.
Trees cut down for too much paper,
That's no good, it wouldn't do any better.
Power stations produce a lot of smoke, polluting the air,
For the whole world it's not really fair.
Leaving rubbish on the floor is bad,
Because if you do Mother Earth will be mad.
Homeless animals are treated with no care,
They have no strength like a lonely bear.

Cardhelle Galapon (11)
Fairfields Primary School, Basingstoke

Our World

Cars are pumping out oil
From the bottom of the car.
I say . . . if you have a bike you should ride it to your work,
But if you live near to your work you should walk.
It will really make a difference.
Please start or our world will be in danger.

Patience Miller (10)
Fairfields Primary School, Basingstoke

The Poverty Poem

When you see people in the street
No money, nothing to eat
Give them a penny
(They don't have too many)
And then they can get a treat.

Paul May-Miller (10)
Fairfields Primary School, Basingstoke

Pollution

Pollution, pollution everywhere,
Stop this pollution 'cause we now have dirty air!

Pollution, pollution,
It's not fair for those animals who live out there!

Stop, pollution causes bad diseases
And it's not fair for us out there!

Kerrie Buchanan (10)
Fairfields Primary School, Basingstoke

Recycle Now

Recycle, recycle before it's too late.
If you do you'll be sure to have a mate.
You've got to act fast, like we did in the past,
If you don't the world won't last.
Come on guys, you know the score,
Don't chuck rubbish on the floor.
Put rubbish in the bin before the pollution starts.
Quickly, before the world breaks all its hearts.

Antony Crosby (10)
Fairfields Primary School, Basingstoke

Recycle Your Rubbish

The world is like a dump.
Animals are dying day and night.
Creatures are dying in the wide open, deadly seas, lakes and rivers
Because of rubbish.
Don't put rubbish on the road and you will be safe.
Recycle rubbish and the world will be a better place.
If you don't recycle, the world will be a gloomy place.

William Sully (10)
Fairfields Primary School, Basingstoke

Pollution

Litter, litter, look left and right
You won't escape the horrendous sight.
Smashed bottles,
Plants choked by fishing nets.
You did this!
You killed this!
Smashed bottles,
Cracked boxes.
You did this!
You killed this!
Litter, litter, look left and right
You won't escape the horrendous sight.
Wrecked beaches,
Polluted seas,
Do you want this?
If you don't *change!*

Luke Watts (10)
Fairfields Primary School, Basingstoke

Pollution

The world is full of rubbish
Animals dying day and night
Creatures are dying in the sea
Rivers and lakes of oil
And bits of boats trapping fish
And don't put rubbish on the road
And everyone will be safe
Recycle your rubbish
And the world will be a better, happy place
If you don't recycle
The world will be a gloomy, dirty place.

Allen Timbol (10)
Fairfields Primary School, Basingstoke

Pollution

Rubbish, rubbish,
Everywhere,
On the floor and in the air.
Cars everywhere,
Gas polluting our air.
Use them less,
Life's too short.
Change your habits,
Walk even more,
What's that smell?
It's in the air,
Pollution, pollution,
Everywhere.
Smoke I smell,
Not very good for the health,
From factories and smokers.
It pollutes our air,
So stop it, it is not fair.
Oh rubbish, oh rubbish,
Don't drop in the sea.
You're killing animals
And a part of me.
Pollution, pollution,
Is in our air,
It is so not fair.
Children, children,
Stop it now,
Pick up your rubbish,
It is not allowed.

Caitlin Cole (10)
Fairfields Primary School, Basingstoke

Pollution Poem

A smelly, smelly, stinky place,
The odour spreading like jam.
With one puff coming from a car,
The air will be affected, gas, gas, gas.
A mass of gas affecting the air.
It's not fair on people who walk.
Why don't we take care of our world?
We should talk about it
And also recycle,
And instead of driving, could cycle or walk.
What will happen to our world?

Danny Schofield (10)
Fairfields Primary School, Basingstoke

Don't, Don't, Don't Use Cars

Pollution is bad for the world
Save the world, take away cars
Start using bikes, skateboards and rollerblades
Save the world, take away cars,
Pollution will take our air away.
So stop using cars today.
Lots of pollution, lots of cars,
You'll never know if it reaches Mars.
Let us be free, don't let us breathe in . . .
Horrible
Smelly
Fumes.

Maddie Vallis (10)
Fairfields Primary School, Basingstoke

Pollution Rap

Help me save the world,
Don't let people ruin the world,
If you see someone, give them a penny,
Then they'll have so many.

If only you understood,
You would be in a big mood,
Why don't you use your might,
So you can turn wrong to right?

Lewis Frewer (10)
Fairfields Primary School, Basingstoke

Recycle, Reuse And Don't Refuse

Recycle, recycle everything
Recycle, recycle anything
Recycle, recycle, save the world
Recycle, recycle, don't refuse!

Reuse, reuse those old shoes
Reuse, reuse those ancient clothes
Reuse, reuse, save the world
Reuse, reuse, don't refuse.

Samantha Pollock (10)
Fairfields Primary School, Basingstoke

Climate Change

Climate change is when the world is becoming warmer
Climate change is because we are leaving the TV on standby
Also leaving your lights on when you don't need to
To stop climate change, please turn your TV off and also your lights.

Luke Bowers (10)
Fairfields Primary School, Basingstoke

Clean Up The Rubbish

C lean up, stay up all night
L et's look for more rubbish
E at up, eat up, clear up, clear up
A nd then pick up the rubbish
N ext day, let's see

U se it
P lease recycle things

P erfect, perfect
L et's try it, get all rubbish, please, please
E at not too much food
A s long as you clean the rubbish up
S ee that pit of rubbish
E at up, eat up, wake up, wake up!

Rebecca Quinn (7)
Heathfield Junior School, Southampton

Earth Is Good!

Earth is good!
Earth is cool!
Earth is the best of them all!
Keep the grass clean,
It is a lovely dream.
Why are birds so clever?
Their feathers are not made of leather.
Earth is good!
Earth is cool!
Earth . . .
It is the best of them all!
Earth is good!

Sapphire Lewis (7)
Heathfield Junior School, Southampton

Save The Planet

P lease save the electricity
L ook after all the recycling
A nd the animals will not die
N ot for long we can help them look after the world
E lectricity is important, but don't use it all the time
T he planet will die, but we can save it if we don't use the car too much because it lets out gas. Turn the lights off when you don't need them. Please don't leave the tap running as well.

Rhonwen Ellis (7)
Heathfield Junior School, Southampton

Save The World

H elp save the planet
E arth is important
L earn to not throw so much on the floor
P lease save the world.

Ellie-Mae Lacey
Heathfield Junior School, Southampton

Untitled

Earth is great!
Earth is cool!
Without it will be the worst of all!

Chloe Wilson (7)
Heathfield Junior School, Southampton

Don't Litter

P lease tidy your litter
L itter is bad, our animals are dying
A nd you can change it from being a mess to tidy
N ever be a litterbug, it is cruel
E veryone litters one time or another
T errible litter. Pick it up, throw it in the bin
S ave our planet because it is going, going, gone!

Cari Ashman (8)
Heathfield Junior School, Southampton

Help The Planet

P ick the litter up and put it in the bin
L itter is bad to drop on the floor
A nybody can pick up litter
N ever drop litter
E verybody help save the planet
T idy up the Earth.

Chloe Wilkes
Heathfield Junior School, Southampton

Care

C are for the world
A mazing world
R ubbish in the bin
E xcellent if you keep the world clean.

Rhianna Saunders (7)
Heathfield Junior School, Southampton

Care

C lean up the planet,
A nimals are dying,
R ubbish - oxygen is going
E arth is going to be gone.

Elli Woodhouse (7)
Heathfield Junior School, Southampton

Earth Is Amazing

Earth is amazing
Earth is good
I like Earth
Because it is good!

Charlie Rattley (7)
Heathfield Junior School, Southampton

Why

Why did they do it? How did it start?
Why did the bombs go off in the middle of the dark?
The children who lived there
Did their parents hold them tight
And say that everything would be alright?
So what happened in the end?
Who won the war?
Well it's all there for you to see,
Far past your front door.

Eden Byrne-Young (11)
Holy Family Primary School, Bristol

Stop Extinction

The ice is melting,
The polar bears are moaning,
The bamboo is growing all around,
Why are there a few pandas prowling on the ground?

The roar of the Bengal tiger barely to be heard,
What's wrong with our world?
Every day there are bad things being heard.

The poachers are killing our courageous creatures
So stop extinction
And begin by asking your teachers.

Bethany Daniels (10)
Holy Family Primary School, Bristol

Eco-Friend

E arth is being affected!
C limate is changing!
O zone layer is getting thinner!

F riends of the Earth are needed!
R ecycling must start!
I ce caps are melting!
E xtinction of animals should stop!
N o more litter!
D isease shouldn't spread!

Joseph Coutts Wood (10)
Holy Family Primary School, Bristol

Litterbug

Don't drop litter.
It can be very, very bitter.
Put it in the bin.
You will have a great big grin.
If you drop litter on the ground.
You're very, very stupid because the police are around,
When you drop litter, you are a real quitter!
So don't drop litter, you don't want to be a quitter!

Matthew Watkins (11)
Holy Family Primary School, Bristol

Homeless

Being homeless isn't fun,
It really isn't good.
We need to act right now
Before they're gone for good.

Help them with food
And any spare money
And hopefully
Soon their lives will become sunny.

Hannah Pring (10)
Holy Family Primary School, Bristol

Saving Energy

Saving energy is really fun,
You get solar energy from the sun.
If you walk to the west,
Instead of driving, you'll be the best.

Ella Wyatt (10)
Holy Family Primary School, Bristol

Help The People With Poverty

People who live in poverty
Don't have homes like you and me.
Sometimes they don't eat at all,
So they just sit there starving by a wall.
We have clothes all fancy and coloured,
They just have a cloth in which they are covered.
Open your eyes and look and see
That the world is full of poverty.

Elena Bull (10)
Holy Family Primary School, Bristol

We All Hate War

War is evil,
As well as deathly,
Bullets flying,
Bombs falling,
All is horrifying in the war,
Tough and challenging,
But everyone working together,
Gives us all hope.

William Duncan-Gibson (10)
Holy Family Primary School, Bristol

My Solution To Solve Pollution

My solution to solve pollution.
Don't have a bath, cut your bills in half.
Do have a shower, you will save power.
Switch off your light, if you don't need it bright.
Don't use your car, if your journey's not far.
Give your hose a ban, use your watering can.
This is my solution to solve pollution.

Jack Scriven (10)
Holy Family Primary School, Bristol

Be Eco-Friendly

Remember this,
Turn off the lights,
Turn off the taps
And don't litter!
Do you know why?
The Earth will probably die.
I know
Because lots of scientists say so.
If you don't
You'll be odd,
Like a pea in a pod.
I do it but you should too!
So get started now!
Before it's too late.

Sydney Fielden-Stewart (10)
Holy Family Primary School, Bristol

Recycling Fun

Hey!
Don't put those tins in the black bin,
Recycle at school, don't be a fool.
Ride your bike as much as you like.
Turn off the taps during the night.
Reuse your paper in art, and use your healthy heart.
You need to be very careful with
Recycling!

Lydia Gillard (10)
Holy Family Primary School, Bristol

Healthy Eating

Apples are red, grapes are blue,
You always wear comfy shoes.
You wear shoes, to the table,
Your pour out soup with a ladle.
Soup is nice and very hot,
You cook it in a pot.
Be careful that what you eat is,
Fruit, veg and any meat.
Don't snack on chocolate that is sweet,
Or your shoulders might just meet.

Ben Green (10)
Holy Family Primary School, Bristol

Saving Our World

To save on water don't have a bath,
Showers instead cut your bills in half.
Turn off the tap to clean your teeth,
Saving energy is really neat.
We must protect our world by all we do,
Reduce, recycle and of course reuse.
Cycle or walk to get from A and B
Leave the car at home, it's fun you'll see.
Let's find a solution
To cut pollution!

Nicole Walsh (11)
Holy Family Primary School, Bristol

It's Really Cool

Don't be a geek, don't be a fool,
Saving energy is really cool.
Close up the windows, close up the doors,
You won't waste heat like this anymore.
Wrap up your fingers, wrap up your feet,
Then you will want to turn down the heat.
Follow the above and you too will be cool,
Saving energy is the new rule!

Jennifer Ashley
Holy Family Primary School, Bristol

War

W orld War I and II were a disgrace,
O ver many a year it was race against race,
R emember do not try to make wars,
R ank smelling gas created blindness and sores,
Y oung as fifteen would actually fight,
I t was dark, damp and cold and what a horrible sight,
N o one enjoyed death and scarlet blood,
G rass was replaced by dirty smelly mud.

W ith bangs going off all the time,
A war is as bitter as a lime,
R ed poppies will grow soon after,
S hattering bombs will not cause laughter.

William Kendall (9)
John Hampden Primary School, Thame

In The Shade Of The Rainforest

In the shade of the rainforest all was calm,
Everything standing arm in arm.
Then suddenly a loud commotion,
It sounded like a whale from the ocean!
It was in fact a man with a saw,
The toucan gave a loud caw.
The man began to cut a tree,
'Stop!' said the monkey as loud as could be.
'We all want you to stop,' said the spider
But all the man said was, 'No you don't understand,
I need this space, it's my land!'

Aysha Saeed (9)
John Hampden Primary School, Thame

War Is Bad

The horror of war makes me sad,
Strong, brave soldiers doing their jobs,
Lying in wait for the next round of bullets.
War is bad!
I wonder if they knew it would be so bad.
Their friends dying in blood-red skies,
What a waste of innocent lives.
War is bad.

James Reilly (9)
John Hampden Primary School, Thame

Earth Question And Answer Poem

'Mum, can you drive me to school?'
'No!'
'Why?'
'Because it causes pollution.'
'How else will I get to school?'
'Walk!'
'Why?'
'Because if more people walk it will save the planet from pollution.'
'Dad, can I go on the bus?'
'No!'
'Why?'
'It causes pollution.'
'How else will I get to school?'
'Walk.'
'But that's what Mum said!'

Eleanor Dickson (10)
John Keble Memorial Primary School, Winchester

How Sad

How sad -
The world is in
Poverty

How angry -
When you see
People dropping litter

How sad -
Global warming
Is increasing

How angry -
When you hear
Animals are dying.

How happy -
Would the world be
If we all helped
Save the environment?

Polly Pyke (10)
John Keble Memorial Primary School, Winchester

Put Your Rubbish In The Bin · Tanka

Help me I'm dying,
Don't stand back and see me cry.
Pick up your rubbish,
Put it into the green bin.
Don't commit a massive sin!

Sophie Patterson (11)
John Keble Memorial Primary School, Winchester

The Recycle Box

(Inspired by 'The Door' by Miroslav Holub)

Go and look in the recycle box:
Maybe there's a ketchup bottle sitting all alone,
Or a jam jar like a window with the sun shining,
Or a wine bottle as clear as the deep blue sea.

Go and look in the recycle box:
Maybe there's a brown sauce bottle lying on the bottom of the box,
Or a water bottle sparkling in the sunlight,
A piece of plastic as clear as a whiteboard.

Go and look in the recycle box:
Maybe there's an old soggy newspaper full of historic news,
An old comic that is ripped up,
A piece of paper that is unwanted and alone.

Go and look in the recycle box:
Maybe there's some tin foil all torn up,
A scrunched-up and ruined cola can.

Go and look in the recycle box,
It should be empty now!

Georgina Ottley (8)
Millbrook Primary School, Grove

The Recycle Box

(Inspired by 'The Door' by Miroslav Holub)

Go and look in the recycle box:
Maybe there's lots and lots of paper weighing a ton,
Or a can of cat food with lots and lots of ants,
Or one piece of paper that weighs the same as an ant.

Go and look in the recycle box:
Maybe there's a paper aeroplane worn out
Just waiting for someone to pick it out,
Or a baked bean can glistening in the sunlight,
A happy birthday card that's still got writing in it.

Go and look in the recycle box,
It is all empty and shining.
The recycle van has just been.

Sophie May Hadler (8)
Millbrook Primary School, Grove

The Recycle Box

(Inspired by 'The Door' by Miroslav Holub)

Go and look in the recycle box:
Maybe there's a scrunched CBeebies magazine,
Or an old newspaper,
Or a shiny glass jam jar.

Go and look in the recycle box:
Maybe there's an empty plastic bottle,
Or a crushed tin can.

Go and look in the recycle box
It is empty,
The recycle van has just been!

Jordan Barker (8)
Millbrook Primary School, Grove

The Recycle Box

(Inspired by 'The Door' by Miroslav Holub)

Go and look in the recycle box:
Maybe there's an old Coke can finished ages ago,
Or a tin of haddock still smelling of the sea,
Or a shiny piece of foil reflecting the light from the moon.

Go and look in the recycle box:
Maybe there's an old pile of newspaper as faded as memories,
Or some cardboard from a birthday package getting lonely,
Or a scribbled exam sheet with every answer wrong.

Go and look in the recycle box:
Maybe there's a milk bottle smelling of slimy sewers.
A wine bottle carrying the groans of a drunken man.
A tomato ketchup bottle as thin as a snake.

Go and look in the recycle box.
It should be lonely,
The recycle van has just been.

Matthew Moran (8)
Millbrook Primary School, Grove

The Recycle Box

(Inspired by 'The Door' by Miroslav Holub)

Go and look in the recycle box:
Maybe there's a fruit juice carton,
Or a tatty old jumper,
Or empty cartons.

Go and look in the recycle box:
Maybe there are shiny jam jars,
Or newspapers ripped up into pieces,
Or an empty Coke can.

Go and look in the recycle box,
It is empty,
The recycle van has just been!

Cameron Faulkner (8)
Millbrook Primary School, Grove

The Green Box

(Inspired by 'The Door' by Miroslav Holub)

Go and look in the green box:
Maybe there's a tatty old sock as holey as gouda,
A scrunched-up piece of tin foil,
Or a quiche tin.

Go and look in the green box:
Maybe there's an old sweater, as old as my grandad,
Or an old torn-up comic,
A soggy daily newspaper.

Go and look in the green box:
Maybe there is a pickled egg tin.

Go and look in the green box,
It should still be full,
The recycle van is here!

Josh King (8)
Millbrook Primary School, Grove

The Recycle Box

(Inspired by 'The Door' by Miroslav Holub)

Go and look in the recycle box:
Maybe there's a wet and soggy newspaper,
Or a cardboard box with drawing on it,
Or a shampoo bottle with shampoo still in it.

Go and look in the recycle box:
Maybe there's a card with my name on it, all scrunched up,
Or my favourite toy all ripped up,
Glass bottle with wine tipping out.

Go and look in the recycle box:
Maybe there's a Bratz comic wet and torn up,
A strawberry carton with mud in it,
A tin can with ice cream in it.

Elen Adshead (8)
Millbrook Primary School, Grove

The Recycle Box

(Inspired by 'The Door' by Miroslav Holub)

Go and look in the recycle box:
Maybe there's a Coke can that's been washed,
Or a pair of socks that smell like rotten eggs,
Or my dad's magazine.

Go and look in the recycle box:
Maybe there's a rat, the garbage men won't take that!
Or a plastic bottle.

Go and look in the recycle box,
It should be empty
The recycle van has just been!

Findlay Kerr (8)
Millbrook Primary School, Grove

The Recycle Box

(Inspired by 'The Door' by Miroslav Holub)

Go and look in the recycle box:
Maybe there's a rusty metal can,
Or a tin as brown as an old cardboard box,
Or a mouldy metal water bottle that was drunk out of months ago.

Go and look in the recycle box:
Maybe there's an old interesting newspaper, new a hundred
                                             years ago,
Or a torn-up book, interesting but old,
A wet soggy comic from last night's rainy day.

Go and look in the recycle box:
Maybe there's a wine glass, which colour, who knows,
An empty cardboard box ripped and battered,
Or a tin foil tray from last nights roast dinner.

Go and look in the recycle box,
It's empty,
The recycle van has just been!

Harry Bowman (8)
Millbrook Primary School, Grove

The Recycle Box

(Inspired by 'The Door' by Miroslav Holub)

Go and look in the recycle box:
Maybe there's an old but shiny baked bean can lying on its side,
Or a pack of tin foil lying there, with spots of mud sprayed over it,
Or a plain tin that was used for pencils still with some broken lead.

Go and look in the recycle box:
Maybe there's a piece of cardboard from a snooker table,
Or a bit of paper with smudged drawing on it,
An old envelope with the stamp misted off by the rain.

Go and look in the recycle box:
Maybe there's a jam jar with mouldy jam in it,
A wine bottle which was a joy to drink from,
A sauce bottle, scrummy and tasty.

Go and look in the recycle box:
Maybe there's an empty packet from an old jacket,
A piece of plastic from an old toy car.

Go and look in the recycle box,
It has been emptied.
The recycle van has just been!

Joe Herbert (8)
Millbrook Primary School, Grove

The Recycle Box

(Inspired by 'The Door' by Miroslav Holub)

Go and look in the recycle box:
Maybe there's a piece of paper all on its own,
Or a piece of cardboard, ready to be used,
Or a tin foil wrapper that's been torn by the dog or cat.

Go and look in the recycle box:
Maybe there's an old tin can crushed, torn and battered to bits,
Or a tin of baked beans as smelly as my dad's sweaty socks,
Or a jam jar sparkling in a spotlight.

Go and look in the recycle box:
Maybe there's a wine bottle as big as a cat
Or newspapers all wet and soggy.
A brown sauce bottle still with brown stains on it.

Go and look in the recycle box:
Maybe there's some tins that are as smelly as anything.
An empty pot washed and cleaned.
A plastic hat for a toy.

Go and look in the recycle box
It is so clean,
The recycle van has just been.

Mollie Rose Davies (8)
Millbrook Primary School, Grove

The Recycle Box

(Inspired by 'The Door' by Miroslav Holub)

Go and look in the recycle box:
Maybe there's a Coke can as lonely as a cloud in the sky,
Or a piece of tin foil losing its shine,
Or a tin can disappearing when you put the lid on the box.

Go and look in the recycle box:
Maybe there's a jam jar as clear as a window.
Or a milk bottle with drips of milk falling out of the bottle.

Go and look in the recycle box:
Maybe there's a stamp as broken as a torn heart in a paper shredder.

Go and look in the recycle box,
It should be clear of rubbish
The recycle van has just been!

Jodie Mathewson (8)
Millbrook Primary School, Grove

The Recycle Box

(Inspired by 'The Door' by Miroslav Holub)

Go and look in the recycle box:
Maybe there's a cracked glass bottle, cracking in the sun,
Or a transparent milk bottle shining in the sun,
Or a dropped, broken glass safely stored.

Go and look in the recycle box:
Maybe there's a wet, muddy newspaper,
Or a scrunched-up newspaper from days gone by.
A ripped dinosaur wrapping paper torn off in glee.

Go and look in the recycle box,
It should be empty.
The recycle van has just been!

Joshua Othen (9)
Millbrook Primary School, Grove

The Recycle Box

(Inspired by 'The Door' by Miroslav Holub)

Go and look in the recycle box:
Maybe there's a spaghetti can still smelling like spaghetti,
Or a soup tin shining like gold,
Or a scrunched-up tin foil like a silver ball.

Go and look in the recycle box:
Maybe there's a smudged newspaper as soggy as a cat that's wet,
Or a shirt worn every day,
A piece of cardboard as dirty as mud.

Go and look in the recycle box:
Maybe there's a tattered jumper, holes like windows,
A milk carton that stinks so rotten,
A plastic bottle with a drop that wasn't drunk.

Go and look in the recycle box,
It's shining clean,
The recycle van has just been!

Bonny Gao (8)
Millbrook Primary School, Grove

The Recycle Box

(Inspired by 'The Door' by Miroslav Holub)

Go and look in the recycle box:
Maybe there's a bean can smelling of last month's tea,
Or a glass sparkling in the sunlit sun,
Or a piece of plastic beading for a jumper.

Go and look in the recycle box,
It should be empty,
The recycle van has just been!

Jasmine Collins (8)
Millbrook Primary School, Grove

The Recycle Box

(Inspired by 'The Door' by Miroslav Holub)

Go and look in the recycle box:
Maybe there's a tin can from years ago,
Or a newspaper and all the words have faded.

Go and look in the recycle box:
Maybe there's an egg carton as soggy as my raincoat,
Or a piece of glass as shiny as diamonds,
A line of cardboard all bent.

Go and look in the recycle box,
Maybe there's a birthday card that should have been used again.
Clothes ripped up by people.
An envelope scrunched up.

Go and look in the recycle box,
Maybe there's some tin foil all ripped apart,
A rotten blank piece of paper thrown away.

Go and look in the recycle box,
It is empty
Because the recycle van has just been!

Tara Bevan (8)
Millbrook Primary School, Grove

The Recycle Box

(Inspired by 'The Door' by Miroslav Holub)

Go and look in the recycle box:
Maybe there's a clear lemonade bottle,
Or two smashed earrings,
Or a rotten piece of gorgonzola.

Go and look in the recycle box:
Maybe there's a big holey, blue smelly sock waiting for you,
Or four torn ribbons in shreds,
A rough bit of paper torn all over.

Go and look in the recycle box:
Maybe there's a green wine bottle,
An eaten apple core,
A pink dirty hair band.

Go and look in the recycle box:
Maybe there's some tins of baked beans,
An empty tomato soup can,
An old newspaper older than my grandad.

Go and look in the recycle box,
It is full of stuff,
We are waiting for the van to come!

Tiana Brady (8)
Millbrook Primary School, Grove

The Recycle Box

(Inspired by 'The Door' by Miroslav Holub)

Go and look in the recycle box:
Maybe there's a comic all ripped up,
Or a piece of tin foil from a ham quiche,
Or a old receipt all scrunched up like a snowball.

Go and look in the recycle box:
Maybe there's a pair of Dad's socks that smell of cheese,
Or last week's soup can glowing like the moon.
An envelope from my birthday.

Go and look in the recycle box:
Maybe there's a newspaper as soggy as the sea,
Or my old battered jumper I've worn for years,
A to-do list all done and dusted.

Go and look in the recycle box:
Maybe there are some tin cans all scrunched up,
An empty jam jar as clear as water,
A plastic toy all broken.

Go and look in the recycle box,
It should be empty,
The recycle van has just been!

Jessica Clark (9)
Millbrook Primary School, Grove

The Green Tub

(Inspired by 'The Door' by Miroslav Holub)

Go look in the green tub,
Maybe there's plastic bottles that could be made into a floor,
Or a sock as holey as Swiss cheese,
A silver can shining like the moon in the sky.

Go look in the green tub,
Maybe there's a letter to my dog, saying 'I love you',
Or my brother's comic, as torn as a ripped paper,
Glass broken, scrapping tins.

Go look in the green tub,
Maybe there's my daddy's old newspaper still looking new.
An old shoe, as soggy as the ocean's sea.
A foil tray from last night's quiche.

Go look in the green tub,
Maybe there's some tin foil broken into pieces.
An empty tomato soup tin, still smelling luscious.
An orange juice carton hanging off the edge.

Go look in the green tub,
It might be empty,
The green truck has just come!

Katie Sheath (9)
Millbrook Primary School, Grove

The Recycle Box

(Inspired by 'The Door' by Miroslav Holub)

Go and look in the recycle box:
Maybe there's a newspaper as soggy as the sea,
Or a bottle lid, as shiny as glass,
Or a metal lid as new as a board.

Go and look in the recycle box:
Maybe there's a tomato can that still smells,
Or a birthday card with a song inside.
A note as new as anything.

Go and look in the recycle box:
Maybe there's a comic as rotten as food,
A sock like a mouldy book.
A jumper like a tatty newspaper.

Go and look in the recycle box:
Maybe there's some tins and a magazine as tatty as a dog.
An empty soup can as shiny as a pen.
A stamp as old as me.

Go and look in the recycle box,
It is empty,
The recycle van has just been!

Lucy Titmuss (8)
Millbrook Primary School, Grove

The Green Recycle Box

(Inspired by 'The Door' by Miroslav Holub)

Go and look in the green box:
Maybe there's an empty see-through Dr Pepper bottle,
Or maybe an old smelly nappy with stains and looking quite damp.

Go and check the green box:
Possibly there's a newspaper, between you and me,
                       it's older than my grandad.

Go and look in the green box:
Maybe there's my brother's dummy, all broken, how sad.

Go and look in the green box,
Maybe there's a plaster smelling like cheese,
Or the family carton of milk.

Go and look in the green box:
Maybe there's the dog's tin of food,
Or the paint from decorating my room.

Go and look in the green box,
It should be empty,
The recycle van has just been!

Jack Cheshire (8)
Millbrook Primary School, Grove

The Green Box

Go and rummage in the green box:
Maybe there's a baked bean can shining on its own like a gold star,
Or a Fanta Fruit Twist can all scrunched up,
Or a birthday card stuck inside my comic I read yesterday.

Go and rummage in the green box:
Maybe there's an egg box which has been drawn on like a picture
                              of someone all coloured in,
Or even a rat eating my favourite cheese yum-yum.
Some cardboard which my dad tried to squash.

Go and rummage in the green box:
Maybe there's a glass bottle with lots of cracks.
A washed-out milk carton with no lid.
An envelope with the sticker ripped off.

Go and rummage in the green box,
Maybe there's a tin of mushy cat food.
I think my neighbour put it in the wrong bin.
An empty hair bottle of blonde hair dye.
A scrunched-up piece of paper with the first draft of this poem.

Go and rummage in the green box,
It should be empty,
The recycle van has just been!

Harriet Talbot (8)
Millbrook Primary School, Grove

The Recycle Box

(Inspired by 'The Door' by Miroslav Holub)

Go and rummage in the recycle box:
Maybe there's a Coke can all washed out,
Or a ripped-up birthday card with 8 on it,
Or a piece of paper with a drawing on it.

Go and look in the recycle box:
Maybe there's a comic, every page read and it has been ripped,
Or yesterday morning's newspaper 2008,
An old smelly football sock with a hole in it.

Go and look in the recycle box:
Maybe there's a sticky stamp with the Queen on it.
A plastic bottle reused for the hundredth time and worn out.
A jam jar shiny as a crystal.

Go and look in the recycle box:
Maybe there's some tin cans all very clean,
A empty big bottle of fruit juice,
A big plastic bag cut up.

Go and look in the recycle box,
It is empty and clean,
The recycle van has just been!

Samuel Hinder (8)
Millbrook Primary School, Grove

The Green Recycle Box

(Inspired by 'The Door' by Miroslav Holub)

Look in the green recycle box:
Maybe there's an envelope all scrunched up,
Or a box of clothes with holes in,
Or a stamp ripped off.

Look in the green recycle box:
Maybe there's a note from a birthday card saying
                    'Happy Birthday Jamie'
Or last week's comic with three ripped pages,
Maybe Mum's magazine filled with recipes.

Look in the green recycle box:
Maybe there's a pair of old boots as wet as a puddle,
A shampoo bottle all nice and sweet,
A milk carton all smelly and rotten.

Go and look in the green recycle box,
It should be full
The recycle van has just got here!

Lee Stone (8)
Millbrook Primary School, Grove

The Recycle Box

(Inspired by 'The Door' by Miroslav Holub)

Go and look in the recycle box:
Maybe there's a bean can as dark as the night sky,
Or a bit of cardboard only used for junk modelling.

Go and look in the recycle box:
Maybe there's a treasure box as wrecked as a shipwreck,
Or a folder as clean as a whistle.

Go and look in the recycle box:
Maybe there's a model aeroplane with a broken wing,
Or an empty envelope as thin as a squashed fly,
Or a ketchup bottle as red as a postbox.

Bethany Cassettari (8)
Millbrook Primary School, Grove

Reuse, Reduce, Recycle Box

(Inspired by 'The Door' by Miroslav Holub)

Go and look in the recycle box:
There's scrunched-up foil from the Sunday roast,
Or a plastic container with a hole in the middle.

Go and look in the recycle box:
Maybe there's a strawberry trifle from last Christmas,
Or a smelly cardboard box.

Go and look in the recycle box,
It's as clean as anything,
Because the recycle van has just been!

Ben Peirce Challenger (8)
Millbrook Primary School, Grove

The Recycle Box

(Inspired by 'The Door' by Miroslav Holub)

Go and look in the recycle box:
Maybe there's a pile of newspapers, read long ago,
Or a pile of newspapers as wet as the sea,
Or a pile of newspapers as old as the hills.

Go and look in the recycle box:
Maybe there's a bean can that still has beans clinging to it,
Or a bean can as shiny as silver,
Or a bean can that is starting to rust.

Go and look in the recycle box:
Maybe there's an old bottle which has not been used,
An old bottle from a party,
A bottle from years ago.

Go and look in the recycle box,
The rubbish shouldn't be there
Because the recycle van has just been!

Matthew Druce (8)
Millbrook Primary School, Grove

The Recycle Box

(Inspired by 'The Door' by Miroslav Holub)

Go and look in the recycle box:
Maybe there's a water bottle sparkling in the sunlight,
Or an unwashed wine bottle reflecting last night's party,
Or a tomato soup can bleeding from inside.

Go and look in the recycle box:
Maybe there's a broken window shattered with a stick,
Or a crushed Coke can with dirty fingerprints inside,
Or a broken elastic band so old, it could be crackled up
                                                        with one touch.

Go and look in the recycle box:
Maybe there's some tin foil crunched in seconds,
An empty baked bean can bounced its way inside,
A smashed pencil pot releasing the writer's tools,
A rotten Lego man saved from the fire.

Go and look in the recycle box,
It should be empty now,
The recycle van has just been!

Robyn Thomas (8)
Millbrook Primary School, Grove

The Recycle Box

(Inspired by 'The Door' by Miroslav Holub)

Go and look in the recycle box:
Maybe there's a Coke can as shiny as cat's eyes,
Or a birthday card as ready for the party as it could be,
Or a cardboard box as clean as when it was delivered.

Go and look in the recycle box:
Maybe there's a pile of toys as good as new,
Or a CD player booming its last part of life,
Tin foil glimmering as the lamp post shines down on it in
                                        the dark night
An old can blinding me with so much glimmering light.

Go and look in the recycle box:
Maybe there's some baked beans rattling like someone's
                                        kicked them,
Or an empty box which makes a good playhouse,
A shimmering light bulb that used to go off.

Go and look in the recycle box,
It must be clean now because,
The recycle van has just been!

Hasan Bahar (9)
Millbrook Primary School, Grove

The Recycle Box

(Inspired by 'The Door' by Miroslav Holub)

Go and look in the recycle box:
Maybe there's a tin as shiny as a silver medal,
Or a Coke can that my brother enjoyed lots,
Or a pile of tin foil ripping very easily.

Go and look in the recycle box:
Maybe there's a newspaper as old as a dinosaur called
                              Tyrannosaurus Rex,
Or a birthday card sent to me in an envelope,
A shiny envelope that was bought for my birthday.

Go and look in the recycle box:
Maybe there's an empty bottle drunk by me,
A jam jar as wonderful as a butterfly,
A nice sauce memory in a tomato ketchup bottle.

Go and look in the recycle box:
Maybe there's some old clothes that I grew out of,
Or an empty plastic bottle leaking at the bottom.

Go and look in the recycle box,
It should be lovely and clean,
The recycle van has just been!

Joe Horton (9)
Millbrook Primary School, Grove

Go And Look In The Recycle Box

(Inspired by 'The Door' by Miroslav Holub)

Go and look in the recycle box:
Maybe there's a dusty can that has been there for a week,
Or a plastic bottle that's been in a fight with a boxer dog.

Go and look in the recycle box:
Maybe there's a metal can, cut in half, waiting to be fixed,
Or wallpaper that looks like a scrunched-up ball,
Or wood waiting to be made into pencils.

Go and look in the recycle box:
Maybe there's a perfume bottle opened with smells of delight,
Or a metal tray lying there from today's dinner.

Go and look in the recycle box:
Maybe there's something shining as bright as ice in the sun,
An empty chocolate box licked clean,
A plastic cup scrunched up like paper that's in a tornado.

Go and look in the recycle box,
A plastic box waiting with boredom and loneliness.
The recycle van has just been!

Lauren Hannah Goodenough (8)
Millbrook Primary School, Grove

The Recycle Box

(Inspired by 'The Door' by Miroslav Holub)

Go and look in the recycle box:
Maybe there's a scrunched-up Coke can,
Or a shiny piece of silver tin foil
Or a baked bean can still smelling of beans.

Go and look in the recycle box:
Maybe there's a massive bunch of paper piled up in front,
Or a bunched up cardboard box right in front of your eyes,
Or a newspaper that has writing like a comic book.

Go and look in the recycle box:
Maybe there's a wine bottle still very shiny,
Or a red tomato sauce bottle still as red as blood,
Or a jam jar as shiny as the sun.

Go and look in the recycle box
It should be a bit sad
The recycle van has just been!

Kurtis Conor Collins (8)
Millbrook Primary School, Grove

The Recycle Box

(Inspired by 'The Door' by Miroslav Holub)

Go and look in the recycle box:
Maybe there's a tin as hard as steel,
Or a Coke can as shiny as silver,
Or a roll of tin foil as scrunched as a leaf.

Go and look in the recycle box:
Maybe there's an old piece of paper as wet as the sea
Or an envelope as damp as a tear,
Or a piece of paper as white as a polar bear.

Go and look in the recycle box,
It should be silver clean,
The recycle van's just been.

Olivia Simpson (8)
Millbrook Primary School, Grove

The Recycle Box

(Inspired by 'The Door' by Miroslav Holub)

Go and look in the recycle box:
Maybe there's a tin can as shiny as silver,
Or a piece of tin foil as scrunched as a ball,
Or a tin as bumpy as gravel.

Go and look in the recycle box:
Maybe there's a torn piece of paper with a jagged edge,
Or a piece of cardboard as bendy as paper,
A glass wine bottle that must have been refreshing.

Go and look in the recycle box:
Maybe there's a Coke can still wet from when it was washed.

Go and look in the recycle box,
It should be empty and clean,
The recycle van has just been.

Harry Roberts (8)
Millbrook Primary School, Grove

The Recycle Box

(Inspired by 'The Door' by Miroslav Holub)

Go and look in the recycle box:
Maybe there's an old baked bean can that's been washed,
Or a macaroni cheese can wrapped in tin foil,
Or a Bob the Builder tin, left over.

Go and look in the recycle box:
Maybe there's a pile of cardboard in the bin,
Or a pile of newspapers as wet as your hair in a storm.
Maybe there's lots of jam jars from a locked-up cupboard.

Go and look in the recycle box
It is clean as a whistle
Because the recycle van has just been.

Jessica Reeder (8)
Millbrook Primary School, Grove

The Recycle Box

(Inspired by 'The Door' by Miroslav Holub)

Go an look in the recycle box:
Maybe there's a smelly dog food can, smelling like tripe,
Or a can or two of beer Dad must have enjoyed,
Or a soup can shining in the sunlight.

Maybe there's a cardboard box that can easily be crafted by me,
Shh! I'll take it before Mum sees!
Or an envelope of Mum's, smiling at me.

Go and look in the recycle box:
Maybe there's a pair of shoes
My fave, I'll have them back definitely.

Go and look in the recycle box:
Maybe there's some tin cans shining like they are blinding me,
An empty jam jar smelling of raspberry jam,
An old damp blanket with the colour fading.

Go and look in the recycle box,
It should be clean,
The recycle van has just been!

Chloe Kilpin (8)
Millbrook Primary School, Grove

The Recycle Box

(Inspired by 'The Door' by Miroslav Holub)

Go and look in the recycle box:
Maybe there's a piece of tinsel shining like the moon,
Or a can dark and gloomy,
Or a tin lid broken like some people split up.

Go and look in the recycle box:
Maybe there's a pile of daily newspapers in a neat pile,
Or an envelope as torn as a broken heart,
Or a bill that costs loads.

Go and look in the recycle box:
Maybe there's a very pretty wine bottle as shiny as a lamp.

Go and look in the recycle box,
It has just been emptied
The recycle van has just been!

Georgina Dawson (8)
Millbrook Primary School, Grove

Rainforests

Rainforests are as beautiful as you!
I saw a man come round with a silver axe.
The trees were gone and so was you!
I felt sorry for the trees.
Trees are gorgeous,
Trees can be dangerous,
Trees make oxygen for us,
Trees are special, I love trees!
Trees may not be here all the time
But they will guide you everywhere you go!
Trees make me feel sunny in my tummy.
It hurts when I don't see trees.

Hannah Emerson (7)
Oakwood Preparatory School, Chichester

Choke

L ooks revolting and smells like sick
I t can kill most of the birds, the sharp can,
 can cut them and they bleed to death.
T rips up the people and the elderly can die
T ime to think about our Earth.
E veryone can make a change, it's not too late.
R ubbish can kill.

Archie Lyndhurst (7)
Oakwood Preparatory School, Chichester

Litter

L ots of smelly litter crumbled on the floor.
I don't like the rotten, smelly rubbish.
T omorrow the whole world will be covered with litter.
T oday we should stop doing it.
E very day we should pick it up.
R espect the times when people have to pick up your rubbish.

Thea Morgan (7)
Oakwood Preparatory School, Chichester

Litter

We are throwing paper bags all over the countryside.
We are also leaving litter on the streets.
We are throwing vegetables in the bin and they are rotting away.
Throw rubbish into the right bin.
The rubbish makes the Earth look like a rubbish dump.
Gas litters the air.
I just hate it when it's dirty.

Noah Chisham (7)
Oakwood Preparatory School, Chichester

The Earth Poem

The world is a sparkling emerald.
Carefully and slowly
It is moving without us knowing.
The skies are as white as pearls.

But look closer:
Factories are spitting out deadly poison
That spreads death and diseases.

It's disgusting, deadly, dirty stuff
Clogging the lungs of our planet,
Until we can't breathe and choke on the air.

We need to open the windows,
Let out the smog
And spring clean the Earth.

We need to pick the scab of factories
From the planet's skin.
We should always love and protect the Earth that we live on.

Polly Williams (8)
Oakwood Preparatory School, Chichester

Pollution

P eople packing planes that zoom through the air.
O nly lorries can hold heavy loads.
L itter spilled everywhere, making our world horrible.
L orries driving on the road, *brum, brum, brum!*
U nbelieveable trains taking passengers around.
T ransporters taking heavy trucks to the garage.
I ncredible caravans going to the sites.
O nly buses can be double deckered.
N asty helicopters flying around, dropping fumes.

Emily Bradford & Ella Johnson (7)
Oakwood Preparatory School, Chichester

A Better World

From the treetops you can look into a wonderful place.
A blanket of green and jade trees.

So as we jump down and look a little closer:

Suddenly we see that the world is not so green;
Trees are missing,
That the clean air is smelling,
The animals are hiding
And people are not so happy.

From the ground you can look into a wonderful place.
Just remember to try and recycle the things you use every day.
Take a car ride with a friend to school
And then you can smell the fresh air
And see our wonderful place down here.

Felicity Davis (8)
Oakwood Preparatory School, Chichester

Pollution

P lease start using bicycles.
O f course cars can be dangerous.
L orries are causing fumes.
L ots of buses are damaging the Earth.
U se cars less.
T omorrow the Earth will be dusty and then we will
                                          not be able to see.
I n the sky a plane makes fumes.
O n the train tracks trains come down.
N o more damaging the Earth.

Abigail Hoskins (7)
Oakwood Preparatory School, Chichester

Homelessness

H omeless people crying out
O nly have themselves for help
M oney, money, where is it? Nowhere!
E verybody, we've got no food except your scraps
L ook over into the rubbish dump
E very eye spies nothing over there
S craps are nothing but a mouldy apple
S tew would be my favourite food
N othing but animal skin is warm
E verything else is cold
S craps are so cold but we have to eat them
S tay alive for as long as we can . . .

Amelia Pope (7)
Oakwood Preparatory School, Chichester

Pollution

P lanes puff out swirling smelly gases.
O n land, Land Rovers puff out stinky smoke.
L orries make nasty smoke.
L ots of cars are making too much misty gas.
U nderground trains puff too many fuel fumes.
T ractors make loads and loads of noise.
I don't like the smell of any of it.
O h the disgusting smell is stinky.
N o more using your car when you don't need to.

Isabel Ebert & Kitty Williams (7)
Oakwood Preparatory School, Chichester

Earth

The Earth is as beautiful as sapphires and emeralds
Glistening in the sunlight as it is rising.
The Earth is as pretty as can be.

Now look closer:
The sky is as dark as a tiger's eye.
The sea is as filthy as a boy playing football and rugby.

The Earth has properties that we are not looking after.
Animals are becoming extinct over the years.

We should stop cutting down trees.
We should stop building factories.
We need to plant more trees and stop polluting.

The Earth is as beautiful as pearls and rose quartz
Shining the light of the sun setting on New Year's Eve.

Katie Wild (8)
Oakwood Preparatory School, Chichester

Pollution

P lanes drop oil whilst flying, swooping low.
O il sticky, gloopy, slimy, spreading everywhere.
L itter, smelly, sticky, looks revolting really.
L ooks slimy very like a blob of glue.
U nder the foot of your shoe or trainer like a stamp.
T ramples over like a giant as big as me.
I n trains the drop out fumes to make pollution.
O ut of the chimney there comes lots of smoke.
N o other people will pollute again.

Johnny Pardey & Hector Small (7)
Oakwood Preparatory School, Chichester

Imagine A World...

Imagine a world without any water,
Imagine a world without any trees,
Imagine a world with nobody living there,
So stop polluting please.

No ice cubes to cool down a drink,
No swimming in the splashy sea,
No bathing in your hot bath,
No fun for you and me.

No paper to draw and colour on,
No birds in a nest in a tree,
No logs to burn on a fire,
Not much fun for you and me.

No parties, no fun, no games,
No people to go and see,
No friendships to make and enjoy,
Nobody here, not even you or me.

Georgina Yeomans (9)
Oakwood Preparatory School, Chichester

What Is Poverty?

P oor people in the dirty, lonely streets calling out for care.
O nly eating rotten, slimy, sticky scraps.
V ery shivery in the winter.
E mpty bins stuffed with wrappers.
R arely is there anything to eat.
T reated badly all their lives.
Y ou imagine life like this.

Bertille Michel & Ellie McDonald (7)
Oakwood Preparatory School, Chichester

Our Earth

E arth is our home, the small quiet planet,
Earth is our life, our only place to stay,
Earth is the best, better than all the rest.

A ngry is our Earth, too much rubbish on the floor,
Annoyed is the air, too much pollution,
Atmosphere is astonished, gloomy, dull, miserable.

R ecycling is best, better than throwing away,
Ruined is the Earth, by daytime work,
Ruined are trees, every single one.

T he bin is there for a reason,
There for rubbish, not the floor,
There are lots of bins around, use them!

H ome is our Earth,
Home is our planet, our universe,
Home is where we are.

Emily Rose (9)
Oakwood Preparatory School, Chichester

Our Earth

Our Earth from space is a glistening, beautiful sapphire spinning.
It is an orb in the middle of the atmosphere.

If you look hard you can see rubbish surrounding cities,
Televisions being left on standby and using our phones
                                      for a long time.
Factories spewing out pollution.
We only have one world and we are destroying it
With lots and lots of wars, using bombs.

We should be protecting our Earth as if it were a scared child.
If it is hurt we put a bandage around our world
And if it is cut we put a plaster on it.

Fergus Bonar (8)
Oakwood Preparatory School, Chichester

Save Our Jewels

The Earth is a sparkling emerald with glittering diamond skies.
Pearl clouds hanging there.
The sea sparkles like blue sapphires.
Our land glows with grass.
The sun looks like a pot of bright shining gold.

But look closer:
We are not looking after our beautiful jewels.
Their brilliant shine is fading away
With our smoking, littering, cutting down trees, burning endless fuel
And building factories.
We are poisoning our planet.
It is getting filthy, disgusting and poisonous.
Take care of our precious pot of gold
Before we young ones are too old.
Stand up, shout, be bold.
'No more polluting and cutting down trees.'
The world is in our hands.

Luke Haddow (8)
Oakwood Preparatory School, Chichester

Beautiful World

The world is a ticking time bomb
Can we save it in time?
We are chopping down trees,
Animals are dying,
Sinking in concrete for factories and houses,
The ice caps are melting because of pollution,
Meanwhile the world is like a ruby glittering in space.
Spinning slowly, silently between the stars and the sun.

Oscar Hughes (8)
Oakwood Preparatory School, Chichester

Our Beautiful World

If you look at a globe,
You can see the Earth and how beautiful it is.
It looks like a sapphire orb with emerald shapes
And we are destroying it very badly.

Look out the window or go outside and you will be surprised,
The Earth is really awful from outside.
Trust me, it is no lie.

A river that used to be as clear as glass, it's now as dark as night.
Factories instead of trees and landscapes,
Loads of cities being built.
It is not a pretty sight.

We should get rid of some of the factories, plant some new trees.
Stop littering and put things in the bin or recycle.
We should look after the world, it is the only one we will get.
We should let its beauty show and one day maybe it will.

Georgia McKirgan (9)
Oakwood Preparatory School, Chichester

We Need To Recycle Our Rubbish

We're killing our world at such great haste,
To help reduce this, we should recycle our waste.

So listen up, I can't say it any plainer,
Put your rubbish in the right container.

Doing our bit for what it's worth,
Fighting the cause to save Mother Earth.

So don't be a chump and put your rubbish in the dump,
Conquer your sin and put it in the recycling bin!

Eloise Flippance (10)
Oakwood Preparatory School, Chichester

Our World

Our world is like a blue and green marble,
Floating around space.
The green bit of marble is sparkly emerald
And the blue part is a shiny sapphire,
But that was when we first saw it.

But we did things there for a long time,
It now looks like a dirty, disgusting rubbish bin
With pollution all around.

Now humans go to the moon,
That will soon be a screwed up piece of paper.

We should leave the moon alone
And spend more time on our own planet
And put a great big plaster on it and put medicine in the sea.

The Earth is like a sparkly emerald
And a shiny sapphire pushed together to make a planet,
The only planet called Earth.

Max Rawlins (8)
Oakwood Preparatory School, Chichester

Stop Polluting Our Land

We are polluting the world.
We are destroying our home and planet.
We throw out litter.
Our land is getting ruined by people manufacturing
    poisonous chemicals which pollute our atmosphere.
Every day people pollute the world.

From space the world looks beautiful and gleams in the sky.
But look carefully, the planet is sinking hard.
We are being nasty to the world and killing things on the planet.
We live on the planet every day.

Emma Russell (8)
Oakwood Preparatory School, Chichester

A Rap For The Planet

Dumping rubbish on the ground
Can release harmful gases all around.

Boom, boom, shsh, boom, boom, shsh
Boom, boom, shsh, boom, boom, shsh

Think of starving kids, they're for real,
Now finish up the rest of your meal.

Boom, boom, shsh, boom, boom, shsh
Boom, boom, shsh, boom, boom, shsh

Computers and mobile phones,
Release radiation – a threat to life on Earth, our home.

Boom, boom, shsh, boom, boom, shsh
Boom, boom, shsh, boom, boom, shsh

Light pollution disrupts the plant habitat,
Will someone tell me, 'What's the reason for that?'

Boom, boom, shsh, boom, boom, shsh
Boom, boom, shsh, boom, boom, shsh

God gave us this wonderful place,
We can save the planet - we are the human race!

Arabella Barwick (10)
Oakwood Preparatory School, Chichester

Save Our World

People everywhere breathe the same air,
Share the same seas and live together on the land.
People everywhere who learn, plan, work, care,
Can save the Earth.
Everyone can save the Earth by . . .
Not polluting, recycling and no more smoking.
That's how we can save our world.

Edward Williams (9)
Oakwood Preparatory School, Chichester

War

War is bad
it makes me
ferociously mad.

Our ears are assaulted
by the screams of bombs
and cries of guns.

People's faces
are streaked with grim tears.

Metal monsters move on their tracks
chewing up the earth beneath
and looking like they're getting ready
to pounce on their prey.
So stop the fighting
and stop the wars
otherwise we will be destroyed.

Jack Congdon (10)
Oakwood Preparatory School, Chichester

Our Planet

O ur planet is our home.
U nder our hands is the world.
R ubbish is making our planet ill.

P rotect our planet and stop digging cuts
   in the Earth's skin with bombs.
L itter is killing our world.
A world is our home and our Earth is glowing for help.
N ow you can act to help the world.
E nd littering and start helping our globe.
T ry and help our planet.

Mattie Hutchings (9)
Oakwood Preparatory School, Chichester

Our World

Our world is a crystal that is blue and green,
Spinning like a disco ball, hanging in the heart of space.
But look closer, loggers are chopping down trees
Like cutting the Earth's love down
And bombs are wounding the Earth's glass skin.
But look closer still, cities are bruising the Earth,
People are littering the world,
Like stones getting chucked at the world
And breaking its precious bones.

We have the world in our hands,
We must take care of our world,
We need to treasure our world.
It's our only hope.

Patrick Langmead (9)
Oakwood Preparatory School, Chichester

Emerald Orb

Our world is an emerald orb glistening in space as it slowly goes by in the sapphire-blue sky and passes the little diamond stars.
But we are building factories like scabs on the Earth's surface.
We're chopping down rainforests and taking away animals' homes.
We're taking the Earth for ourselves and thinking about nobody else.
We're spewing litter onto our Earth.
We need to put shields around the factories, plant trees back into our world and wipe up all our mess.
If we did this God's world would once again be a beautiful place
                                                           to live in.
Then we could enjoy our emerald orb.

Francesca Coulson (8)
Oakwood Preparatory School, Chichester

War

War destroys homes,
War kills trees,
Because of war,
There's only you and me.

War is not great,
War is a fight,
I can't sleep during the night.

War is like hell,
If you're put in a cell,
With a terrible smell.

Tanks pollute the air,
Right above your hair.

War is bad,
It makes me sad,
All this bombing makes me mad.

So stop the war,
Go away,
War was yesterday.

Luke Connell (10)
Oakwood Preparatory School, Chichester

Save The Earth

Don't throw litter because animals think it's bitter.
If we keep polluting, then God will fire the sun
And we will have to run.
Stop cutting trees down, it really upsets the bees.
Polar bears have no ice; we are tearing their home apart.
Stop polluting oceans,
The creatures that live there have to inhale the horrible potion.
We need to save the Earth. The world is our home.

Zoe Barnett (9)
Oakwood Preparatory School, Chichester

Our World

Our world may be small
But it is the best
Because it is like a jewel
Spinning round and round like a ballerina
But we ruin it by riding a motorbike,
We run around like a deadly warrior
Waiting to destroy the world by murder
Litter
Litter
Everywhere
City
City
Everywhere
We should have left the world the way it was
Then it would be nice and peaceful
No destruction
Heal the world
Help the world
What you put in it what you get
Cradle the world

Make an army
Re-grow the world

Save the world
From death.

Jasper Jellett (9)
Oakwood Preparatory School, Chichester

Our World

Our world is a treasure
That shines at midnight
With gorgeous blue and green jewels.

Our world is a magnificent
Watercolour splashed jewel
Like a star hanging in space.

But look closer:
Rubbish is scouring the cities
Like a swarm of termites.

All the cars pollute the jewel
Like a hurricane
Scouring the globe.

This is our only home.
We should love it
With our minds.

It is a jewel
That needs us to love it
And care for it like a baby.

We are lucky
To have a world
As beautiful as this.

Heal our world. It is a treasure
That shines at midnight
With gorgeous blue and green swirls.

Remember to look after it.

Jaime Pardy (9)
Oakwood Preparatory School, Chichester

The Shimmering Diamond

The Earth
Is a brilliant pearl-sized diamond
In the gigantic mines of space
But look closer
The black warriors of litter, war, disease and poverty
Are roaming around and their army is nearly here!
There is a smoke hovering
Around the diamond
We have the world in our hands
And should destroy the black warriors
And their army
By gathering armies of bushes and trees
Polish the diamond
And it will reward you
By displaying its fantastic beauty it once had.

Lloyd Morgan (9)
Oakwood Preparatory School, Chichester

Our World

Our world is like a shiny balloon,
Bobbing up and down around the moon.
We should help our world win
Or one day it will turn into a big rubbish bin.
Our world is like a fireball,
It makes light and warmth within us all.
If we don't keep our world safe
Animals will die and homes will be destroyed.
Pollution will be floating in the air,
Killing birds and creatures there.
Our world helps us live with water and food,
It puts us in a jolly good mood.
So we must all take care of this wonderful place
And keep it safe for the future race.

Ella Small (9)
Oakwood Preparatory School, Chichester

Littering

We think it's so fantastic,
How everything comes wrapped in plastic,
It makes the animals sad
And it makes the world go mad.

The growth of all this litter,
Is making the animals very bitter,
We litter because we are lazy,
But if we think about it, we're really crazy.

The reason why we are crazy to mess,
Is the number of animals are getting less,
They all do something quite distinct,
But they can't help us if they are extinct.

The animals are calling,
So don't act so appalling,
Please remember my poem and don't forget it,
Because if you keep littering you're going to regret it!

Alexander McKirgan (10)
Oakwood Preparatory School, Chichester

Plastic Bag

While we are shopping, we have all done it,
We have dropped a plastic bag.
The wind picks it up and blows the bag right out,
Out into the sea,
A gull, that poor gull gets tangled up and waits for hours on end,
A fisherman comes by and scoops the bird up,
Then he takes it home and sets it free,
For that is where the gull is meant to be.

Bethany Williams (10)
Oakwood Preparatory School, Chichester

The World

Our world is a blue and green pearl
Hanging like a glitter ball in space
With stars like a million candles – but look closer
Cities are being built on all the amazing forests and killing animals
And combatants are bombing
And bruising the colourful skin of the world
The skin is getting pavements all over it – horrid black stuff
Our world will not be colourful anymore

We have the world in our hands
Let us get armies of tigers, lions, elephants and monkeys
With coconut bombs to fight the pollution
The world is in our hands
We must fight back for that amazing pearl of colour.

Jake Goosen (10)
Oakwood Preparatory School, Chichester

Homeless People

People sleeping on the streets,
Unfortunately for them they have no sheets.

They have no shelter, they have no food,
This always puts them in a bad mood.

They are too dirty to be offered work,
So in the shadows they are forced to lurk.

They sometimes turn to drink and drugs
But they'd probably prefer more hugs.

Look after these people, don't be rude
And put them in a better mood.

Katie Twist (10)
Oakwood Preparatory School, Chichester

A Rubbish Poem

By dropping your litter, or dropping a can,
You're part of pollution, why yes, you!
Don't waste resources, it just isn't fair.
The world is so precious, we must take some care.

Remember, animals inhabit this Earth too, if you didn't realise.
So next time you're out and about, make sure you don't litter.

Litter is a crime and is quite hard to rhyme.
Litter is bad and that makes me sad.

Litter is damaging and it isn't nice to see,
Just put it in the bin instead of doing sin,
It's really easy, honest!
So don't be bitter and don't drop litter.

Ben Taylor (10)
Oakwood Preparatory School, Chichester

Our Earth

O ur atmosphere is dying from poisonous gases.
U se your brain to stop this destruction.
R ealise that we must stop cutting trees down.

E arth is our home and we're putting it under siege.
A ll attackers of the Earth should be punished.
R uin the Earth with atrocious, awful atom bombs and you'll regret it.
T he Earth is a giant sapphire with bits of emerald stuck in it.
H ateful humans loathe the Earth.

James Webber (9)
Oakwood Preparatory School, Chichester

Stop Destroying Our World!

Our world is like a bomb, the time is running out,
It's full of rubbish and garbage, we have to sort it out.

We have to stop dropping so much litter,
Or our world will end up so bitter.

Everyone's got to work as a team
And stop the factories from polluting the stream.

We have to stop watching so much TV,
Turn off the lights and don't waste electricity.

Every single place I've been,
I've been astonished at what I've seen.

I turn around, there's litter there,
I just think some people don't really care!

Georgie Carter (10)
Oakwood Preparatory School, Chichester

Stop Pollution

Pollution is a terrible thing,
Pollution makes the world spring.
For pollution we need a solution,
Pollution has to be reduced.
People from around the world should realise and open their eyes.
Don't make it worse,
The ozone might just burst.
If you stop damaging the Earth,
We will give you a first!

Elliot Ebert (10)
Oakwood Preparatory School, Chichester

Pollution

P ollution
O zone
L itter
L andfill
U nlucky polar bears
T urn off lights to
I mprove the environment
O xygen
N uclear missiles.

Laurie Emerson (10)
Oakwood Preparatory School, Chichester

Felling

F ires burning, destroying all our land.
E xciting if the world could change.
L opping loggers killing trees even though the world says please.
L ogs are being taken down the stream.
I n the rainforest people cut down trees.
N o one cares about our land and especially our trees.
G o and save our land, come on help!

Jonathan Furniss & Philippa Noble (8)
Oakwood Preparatory School, Chichester

Stop Litter

L ove our world.
I mprove our environment.
T ake away some power plants.
T urn off the TV when you're not watching it.
E nvironmentally friendly.
R euse cans and plastic.

Fred Thomas (10)
Oakwood Preparatory School, Chichester

War

War changes lives
War ruins lives
You cannot fix them

Shouting and screaming
Bangs and bombs

War changes countries
War ruins countries
You cannot fix them

Buildings on fire
Destroying our empire

War changes lives
War ruins lives
You cannot fix them

The fog is in the air, the fog is in the way
If you go, it won't stay

War changes countries
War ruins countries
You cannot fix them

It makes you want to scream and shout
And leaves a bitter taste in your mouth

War changes lives
War ruins lives
How can we fix them?

Bobby Filary (10)
Oakwood Preparatory School, Chichester

Litter

All we see is litter
down to town, on my way
to the dustbins every day.

All we see is litter
on the roads, in the streams
litter running to the sea.

All we see is litter
killing animals fast and quick
let's not forget to clear up quick.

All we see is litter
recycle, recycle without delay
improve our world for another generation to play.

All we see is litter
don't be a litterbug
go green and clean, home and away.

All we see is litter.

Bronte Popplewell (10)
Oakwood Preparatory School, Chichester

The Dying World

The ozone layer is being destroyed by gases.
When the ozone layer gets destroyed we will all die.
The horrible factories and metal cars let off these gases.
The world is dying!
Try and walk around, don't drive.
Try and make objects by hand.

The world is dying, try and save it,
Try your hardest to save the world!

David Brimecome (10)
Oakwood Preparatory School, Chichester

How Many Years Till I'm Extinct?

A loud, loud noise, what could it be?
A chainsaw eating my favourite tree,
I really don't feel they are thinking of me,
My future life I cannot see.

What shall I do? Does it end today?
My mother fights for life, but still she lays,
So I swing down, is she OK?
Is there really no other way?

These selfish humans, hearts made of stone,
I hate these animals destroying my home,
My mother cries, then gives a moan,
She is dead; I'm all alone.

If you're here to fell a tree,
Do please stop and think of me.

Amy Frost (11)
St Alban's CE Primary School, Havant

A Walk In The Park

Cans and bottles blowing around,
Chewing gum spread all over the ground,
Paper, card and much, much more
Is scattered all over the messy park floor.

Pick it up, don't be a slob!
Don't leave it to me, it's not my job.
I'd like a world that's pure and clean,
All I want is a beautiful, natural scene.

Emily Frost (9)
St Alban's CE Primary School, Havant

Rainforest

R ainforests are extraordinary.
A ll the amazing trees over a thousand years old.
I t is home to Indians.
N ew fresh rain every morning.
F orests are homes too,
O ver half our world's animals.
R ainforests are extraordinary.
E veryone should enjoy them.
S o don't destroy them.
T rees, trees, trees so tall, don't cut them down.

Daisy Wiggins (9)
St Alban's CE Primary School, Havant

Giant Panda Gets Annoyed

The rainforest is mine,
Don't waste our time,
Leave my bamboo,
I need it more than you.
Stop cutting it down,
It will make us all frown.
You take our food,
You'll put us in a bad mood.
You kill the tree,
You kill me!

Daniel Aspey (10)
St Alban's CE Primary School, Havant

The Rainforest

In my world it's green and pretty,
Where the monkeys and the big kitty
Would sit and have fun all day,
If I had things my own way.

But truly in real life,
People take a massive knife,
Then they take a chop without a care,
Are you in some kind of dare?

They cut the trees from left to right,
We hear the chainsaws day and night.
Animals are losing their homes all around,
As trees come tumbling to the ground!

Georgina Mellor (10)
St Alban's CE Primary School, Havant

Invisible Bear

Being a polar bear,
Just isn't fair.
My world is melting,
It's getting so hot,
But my thermal coat isn't melting.
There's no one left so now I'm lonely,
My home has gone so I'm dishomely.
It's all disappearing before my eyes,
This is a land of sadness and sighs.
So here I am all lost and alone,
All I want is to go back home.

Johanna Horsman (10)
St Alban's CE Primary School, Havant

Racism

I wake up
Then go to school.
People say 'get lost' or 'go back to where you came from'.
I spend the day having the micky taken.
One man could have changed it for us
But then he got shot down
And now us blacks annoy the whites.
I want to move back to my homeland.
I'm walking home then the bottle smashes.
I'm unconscious till 9 o'clock.
I reach home then my mother says,
'Where have you been all this time?'
I walk straight past her to cry my eyes out in my bedroom.
If only I had had a dream.

Joseph Walsh (11)
St Alban's CE Primary School, Havant

Extinction

E lephants may be big, but are still really rare.
eX tra animals are what we need to save this planet from disaster.
 T igers are in need, help them please.
 I nsects might disappear, is that fair?
 N ever to see a rhino again.
 C an we save the dolphins?
 T urtles are hunted for their skin, surely that must be a sin.
 I guanas need sun to stay alive.
 O rang-utans make homes in trees.
 N ever too late to act.

Samuel Horsman (8)
St Alban's CE Primary School, Havant

Animals In Danger

It used to be cold now it is hot enough to scold,
My home is so hot
Should I be here? Should I not?
I am a polar bear, please help me.

I am an antelope, a bit like a deer,
But the hunters are coming with their rifles and spears.
My friends, the African animals aren't that bad,
But these people are really making me sad.
I am an antelope, please help me.

I am a turtle, a leatherback in fact.
These beachgoers are hurtful to be exact.
They sit on my young, and the young they don't sit on
Are sometimes flung back into the sea,
I am speaking for the turtles, please save us!

Nicholas Robertson (10)
St Alban's CE Primary School, Havant

Litter

Litter, rubbish on the ground,
Different places to be found,
It makes me mad
Because it's bad.
There is litter all around,
So if you see some on the floor
Don't just walk away and ignore,
Pick it up and put it in,
A green environmental rubbish bin.

Claudia Rowthorn (8)
St Alban's CE Primary School, Havant

Disappearing

In the rainforest there's a rasping sound
Of saws whirring round and round
Cutting into all the trees
Sawdust flying in the breeze.

Then all the monkeys at the top
Suddenly hear a great big chop
The trees come crashing to the ground
Landing with an almighty pound.

The monkeys now have nowhere to go
There is nothing but devastation below
As the forests disappear
Extinction threatens, there's no future here.

Amy Shepherd (10)
St Alban's CE Primary School, Havant

Litter, Litter

Litter, litter, why are you there?
On the ground is just not fair,
To help our planet and keep it safe,
It should be put in a better place.
Litter, litter, why are you there?
Gum under benches is just not fair,
Sweet wrappers, cans, bottles and more,
Should all be kept safely in the bin
And not on the floor.

Francesca Chalk (9)
St Alban's CE Primary School, Havant

Litter

Litter, litter on the floor
I can't stand it, don't throw more
Animals die of this bad thing
So don't just sit there, don't just sing
Empty bottles, empty cans
Cut your fingers, cut your hands
Graffiti sprayed all about
Now that is bad without a doubt
Bubblegum sitting on the ground
Sticks on your shoes withoul a sound
So now you hear what I say
Pick up your litter every day!

Catherine Williams (8)
St Alban's CE Primary School, Havant

Litter

Someone named Jan
dropped a sharp, broken can.
There was some sharp glass
hiding in the grass.
Someone named Jeanette
dropped a cigarette.
A little boy dropped some chewing gum,
a panda thought someone's birthday had come
and put it into his tum-tum,
and then it made him run.

Andrew Briggs (7)
St Alban's CE Primary School, Havant

One Step By One

We're destroying our animals.
Yes, destroying our animals.
One step by one.
Save our animals, one step by one.

We're destroying our rainforests.
Yes, destroying our rainforests.
One step by one.
Protect our rainforests, one step by one.

We're destroying our human race.
Yes, destroying our human race.
One step by one.
Care for the human race, one step by one.

We're destroying our world.
Yes, destroying our world.
One step by one.
Save our world, one step by one.

Harrison Blake Martin (7)
St Alban's CE Primary School, Havant

Litter Everywhere

People throwing away their trash
It lands with a noisy crash
Jagged ends of sticky brown glass
End up in the long green grass
Chewing gum thrown on the street
Sticks to everybody's feet
What a nuisance, what a mess
Let's try to do it less.

Julia Martin (7)
St Alban's CE Primary School, Havant

Extinction

When considered,
All in all
With tales long
And tales tall
Have you ever wondered how
Many animals are left now?
A tree's friends
Lie down slain,
Never to get up again
And how many whales
Can still try
To swim back home
To dive and cry?
But you can never blame the solar flares
For wounding all the polar bears.

So you can . . .
Protect the rainforests,
Stop the hunters,
Save the world's
Natural wonders.

Isaac Morgan (8)
St Alban's CE Primary School, Havant

Polluted Seas

Rubbish, litter everywhere,
No one seems to really care.
They don't recycle, they don't reuse,
All they do is let nature lose.
Dolphins, birds, whales and fish,
Are dying out, not our wish.
If everyone tidied their litter
The world would be a lot fitter.

Toby Bunting (7)
St Alban's CE Primary School, Havant

In The Future

In the future
Plastic bags might float in the road
In the future
Gum might sit on benches
In the future
Cigarettes might be squashed on school playgrounds
In the future
Glass might be in the park.

So in the future
Put your litter in the bins
To make the world a better place!

Alice Kaminski (10)
St Alban's CE Primary School, Havant

Litter Is Bitter

Flooding seas,
Chopping down trees,
We are like hunters killing the world.
Empty cans,
Broken down vans,
Suffocating smoke,
Making birds choke.
Animals dead, without a bed.
Stop, think and save our planet,
It's up to you to do your bit.

Matthew Johnstone (7)
St Alban's CE Primary School, Havant

Litter

Broken smashed-up glass
Buried deep in the thick green grass
When kids come out to play
They cut their hands, they don't have a say.

Plastic bags on the side of the bend
Little animals suffocating
It's all our fault
We really need to try and save them.

And how will it be when the dumps are full
With stuff that's been found in a skip?
And why should we panic
As long as it's not our house that goes up on the tip?

Matthew Lee (10)
St Alban's CE Primary School, Havant

In A Couple Of Years

In a couple of years,
There won't be anymore rainforests standing.
In a couple of years,
There'll be no more roars.
In a couple of years,
There'll be no more macaws.
In a couple of years,
There won't be any bogs.
In a couple of years,
There won't be anymore tree frogs.

Alfie Simms (9)
St Alban's CE Primary School, Havant

What Did I Do?

What did I do wrong?
Only swinging from tree to tree?
What did I do to you?
Trying to live my life!
What did I do to get this?
To see men hunt monkeys!
What did I do to get a visit from you?
Eating what I find!
What did I do to be like this?
Nothing, except I'm different from you!

Bronwyn Flower-Bond (11)
St Alban's CE Primary School, Havant

War

Men dying, children crying
Parachutes coming down
Landing in the crowded town
Guns are going off
Making people start to cough
Chucking it down with rubbish rain
Mothers crying in lots of pain
Trees blowing in the breeze
Making people start to freeze
The green fence wire
Alight with orange fire.

Katherine Shepherd (7)
St Alban's CE Primary School, Havant

Alone

Why do we fight and kill each other?
Why do we even have to bother?
Is it religion that is so bad,
It makes us fight and kill and be sad?
Look at those soldiers over there,
What have they done to you, don't glare,
Just because they have different views
Why does it have to become headline news?
I am left all alone now,
No mum, no dad, oh why? And how?
Just because you wanted them dead,
I will now, no longer be fed . . .

Madeleine Spice (10)
St Alban's CE Primary School, Havant

Litter

Left lying in the streets,
Grabbing hold of anything it meets,
Eating away at the things you left,
Free of charge even though it's theft.

People getting hurt from your rubbish,
That's where rats will flourish,
So just look after our world,
Stop and think and don't let our world unfurl.

Mollie Griffiths (10)
St Alban's CE Primary School, Havant

In The Park

Chewing gum covered in spit
Tell that lady not to sit!
Crisp packets blowing in the wind
Why wasn't that beer can binned?
The pond is full of dead fish
Put your dirty rubbish in the bins. I wish!
Walking along you'll get stuck to the floor,
Why did you do it? I say, no more!

Imogen Walsh (9)
St Alban's CE Primary School, Havant

Warning!

People, people, look at our world,
Think what you're doing, what's starting to unfurl.
The Tasmanian wolf, the quagga and dodo,
Extinct forever, because of Man, oh!
We've been so silly, we've been so foolish,
In our oceans we'll soon have *no fish!*
Stop pollution and global warming,
Save our animals, heed my warning.

Olivia Letchford (7)
St Alban's CE Primary School, Havant

Stop The Litter!

By all the waters around,
There are tin cans and plastic bags,
Please stop the litter now!
For it is really bad,
It kills our beautiful animals,
So stop the litter now.

Chloe Anderson (9)
St Alban's CE Primary School, Havant

Extinction

Animals dying,
Hunters lying,
Killing nature all around.

Rhinos going,
Dolphins flowing,
Out of all existence.

Hunters heaving,
Tigers leaving,
Grabbing their lives away.

Pandas going,
Whales flowing,
Out of all existence.

Archie McKeown (8)
St Alban's CE Primary School, Havant

Litter, Litter

Litter, litter, do you like it?
Litter, litter, I really hate it!

Crisp packets in the park,
Floating round in the dark.
Abandoned needles, bits of glass,
Lying quietly in the grass.

Overfilled bins, it's on the telly,
Rotten maggots, phew, it's smelly.

Recycle, reuse or throw away,
Save our planet for another day.

Euan Bonnar (8)
St Alban's CE Primary School, Havant

The World Is Dying

Cardboard, plastic, recycle it all
Or the mountains will start to fall.
The weather is changing as the days go by,
And then the whole world will start to fry.
Rainforest, rainforest, please come back,
Or the Earth will start to crack.
Diseases are spreading very, very fast,
Think back in time, through the past.
There are thousands of things that we are doing,
That are killing the world as I am singing.
Smoke, smoke, horrible smoke,
That is the thing that is making us choke.

Joseph Owen (8)
St John's Priory School, Banbury

Rainforests

R ainforests can be saved by not cutting trees down
A nd animals die because of this.
I ncluding birds, monkeys, chimpanzees and orang-utans
N ormally we cut down so many trees,
F orests are disappearing fast, help save them.
O pen gaps in rainforests are bad,
R ain helps them grow and we then get oxygen
E very rainforest is in danger,
S ome days are rainy and make them grow,
T rees are living things and can breathe,
S ome trees are different.

Lucy Shields (8)
St John's Priory School, Banbury

Recycle Poem

R ecycle, recycle, it is a good thing to help our environment
E very day people recycle but some people don't so if
   we encourage more people to do so we can save our planet.
C an you do it? Of course you can,
   if you do it you're saving our environment.
Y ou should recycle, it's good for our planet.
C ould you please recycle please.
L eave normal bins and recycle.
E very day humans should recycle.

Joshua Kearns (8)
St John's Priory School, Banbury

Rainforest

Rainforest trees must stop being chopped down
We lose oxygen when every tree is chopped down
Trees die and there is less oxygen for us to breathe
We can use both sides of the paper
To save trees being chopping down.

Sean Daniels (8)
St John's Priory School, Banbury

Save The World

Save natural resources and use less paper.
Reduce landfill and recycle.
Stop pollution and use less oil.
Use less aeroplanes, walk to school.
Save energy and help the world.

Thomas McGonagle (8)
St John's Priory School, Banbury

Recycle

R ubbish can be recycled did you know!
E xcept litter goes in the litter bin.
C ans can be recycled!
Y ou can make the world a better place.
C ome on and win the recycle cup!
L itter, litter go away and stay away!
E arth needs you so start . . .recycling today!

Dylan Patel (8)
St John's Priory School, Banbury

Recycle

R ecycle and the world will be a better place
E very bit counts when you are recycling.
C ans and other metals or paper
   can do a lot even though they are small.
Y ou can recycle a lot of things.
C ars and lorries might be recycled.
L ots other bits of metal can help.
E arth is going to end! Please help us fast.

Meera Mahesh (8)
St John's Priory School, Banbury

Recycle

R ecycle your rubbish, return not to the dump.
E xcellent, your rubbish has not gone to the dump.
C artons and packages are made into the new stuff.
Y ou can help the Earth to not get full.
C ardboard and metal are made to make things
L ike cans and springs and things that we need.
E verybody can help to clean the Earth up.

Stephen Marsden (8)
St John's Priory School, Banbury

The World

Don't worry about the fuel cost,
Bio-fuel is coming
So are electric cars
So don't worry.
Some diseases are very painful, like cancer
But the doctors are nearly there.
Have you noticed the war in Afghanistan?
362 British soldiers have died so far.
Do worry about the war.

Harris MacPherson (8)
St John's Priory School, Banbury

What Is Changing?

Poor people are suffering because they don't have any food.
They don't have much shelter or money either.
War. Why do we need war? Why can't they just share oil out?
Please stop people getting bullied, it isn't fair.
Diseases are killing people every day.
How can we help? Recycle.
If you don't recycle the land will fill up with rubbish,
It will be horrid and people will get ill.

Emilia Fletcher (8)
St John's Priory School, Banbury

A Kind Poem

Be kind, be generous, be happy for who you are,
Don't feel scared, you always have someone to talk to.
If you feel like you are always being left out and are very lonely
All you have to do is ask for some attention.

Taya Eames (9)
St John's Priory School, Banbury

Recycling Paper

Recycle paper so it can be made into new paper.
Don't put it in the bin
So you can look after trees.
Don't rip paper up if something goes wrong,
Use the back of pieces of paper.
Don't use too much paper.
Use scrap paper.
Don't draw something if you don't need it.
Try to stop people cutting down trees.
Pick up litter that has been thrown on the ground.
Recycling paper is fun.
Try to save the world.

Emma Robinson (8)
St John's Priory School, Banbury

The World Under Sapphire Seas

Forgotten lands covered by sparkling sapphire seas
Bubbles popping on the surface from buildings below.

Once was crowded but now lonely water-covered seas
What was a human place
Now is ruled by fish emerging from windows.

Sand stretched roads once covered with cars
Now as silent as the desert.

The people should have listened
To the politicians and the newsreaders.

They took advantage to ignore
So nature took revenge on the cities by flooding them.

Alex Hoad (10)
St Lawrence CE Primary School, Lechlade

Haikus

Wars are dangerous.
Gunpowder affects people.
Sadly people die.

Forests are cut down.
Now they have almost vanished.
Birds have lost their homes.

I can see rubbish.
Litterbugs have made it all.
They should clean it up.

Stop that hunting now.
You do not want to be shot.
The poor animal.

The oceans suffer.
Now fish are dying quickly.
Save the oceans, quick!

Sam Plank (9)
Sibford Junior School, Banbury

Green

Turn off the lights.
Green is for leaves.
Stop cutting down trees.
Green is for moss that grows.
Turn off the TV.
Green is for grass.
Turn off the old world.
Green is for seaweed.
Turn the heating off then your bill will not be big.
If you don't we will die.
Save the world.

Amelia Proud (10)
Sibford Junior School, Banbury

Haikus

Industry
Dirty factories
Puffing out black toxic smoke
Making pollution!

Cutting down forests
Killing animals
Forests are becoming less
Causing extinction!

Poaching
It's very cruel
To innocent animals
We have to stop!

Joseph Roxburgh (9)
Sibford Junior School, Banbury

Haikus

Only hunt for food
Animals die everywhere
So no extinction.

Littering angers
Me. Diseases the water
The Earth is weeping.

Wars are heartbreaking
So is death. Families don't
Want it. Stop fighting.

George Woolley (9)
Sibford Junior School, Banbury

Environmental Haikus

I am hunting them.
They are not hard to hunt for.
I can hear them now.

I went to the shop,
To get some oil, the price's
Very high, not fair.

The credit crunch is
On my nerves, things cost a lot,
Bread is far too much.

I had a disease,
I was sick on Friday night,
I felt very ill.

Darcey Mae Rivers (9)
Sibford Junior School, Banbury

My Poem

I am a tree.
The axe men come every week
And take my friends from me.
Slowly I am the last here.
Every time the axe men come in their trucks
And I hear *brrr brrr*
Zzzzzzzzzzuuuooo
I dig my roots in and hope they won't take me.

Sidney Ocanigil-Tunstall (10)
Sibford Junior School, Banbury

Litter

Litter, rubbish,
Waste and trash.
I feel sad.
It pollutes the world.
It's smelly.
It's dirty.
You need to recycle
Make new things
It's better for the world
Than just putting in the bin.

Jack Brooks (7)
Sibford Junior School, Banbury

Environmental Haikus

Littering could change
If all of us recycled
Earth is disgusted

Hunting is cruelty
To innocent animals
Causes extinction.

Dirty water kills
People who have nothing else
Earth is horrified.

Ben Taylor (9)
Sibford Junior School, Banbury

Recycle

Don't throw rubbish
It's bad for the environment
Put your rubbish
In the recycling bin.
Paper makes new books
Tins make new cans
Plastic makes new clothes
Recycle it all.

Henry Jackson-Wells (7)
Sibford Junior School, Banbury

Haikus

Rubbish everywhere
Messy, dirty, horrible
Helpless, disgusted.

Crime makes me feel sick
Makes people feel all ashamed
Of one another.

Hannah Gardiner (9)
Sibford Junior School, Banbury

You!

Use your brain
To get on the train.

Use your bike
Instead of your car
And save the environment.
You could do this!

Orla Gay (10)
Sibford Junior School, Banbury

Environmental Haikus

Hunting is causing
Extinction so please stop now
Animals will die.

Industry makes the
Atmosphere polluted and
Very hot as well.

Thomas Banbury (9)
Sibford Junior School, Banbury

Rubbish

Don't put trash in the bin.
Rubbish can be made
Into something new.
Some things you like
Could be made out of junk.
Recycling is good.

Michael Rae (7)
Sibford Junior School, Banbury

Environmental Haikus

Oceans in danger,
Sealife has changed in a way,
Species dying out.

Every day I sway,
Every day I play with fish,
I love to stand still.

Beth Hughes (10)
Sibford Junior School, Banbury

Environmental Haikus

Stop people hunting
Extinction happening now
Don't, they are like us.

Toxic poisoning
Animals and other things
Depressed, sick inside.

Shouting, explosions
Innocent people dying
Countries torn apart.

Don't kill rainforests
Everything there has a heart
Think of their feelings.

Parris Pratley (9)
Sibford Junior School, Banbury

The Environmental Rap!

Yo!
Do turn off the lights,
So that it's not bright.
Don't use the car anywhere that's not so far.

Yo!
Pick up the rubbish, else when you look in the mirror,
You'll see yourself as disgusting garbage!
Listen to the environmental programme on the TV
'Cause this is important to you and me.
Do not waste electricity, as you and me
Will regret it for the bill on electricity.

Holly Martin (10)
Sibford Junior School, Banbury

Saving Electricity

When you go shopping
And you leave the TV on, turn it off.
When you go downstairs
Don't put the lights on,
Open the window shutters.
Don't leave the lights on for a long time.
When you go to the shops
Turn everything that's electric off.
Don't waste electricity.

Joseph Raybould (7)
Sibford Junior School, Banbury

The Environment

I can smell the smell of a bonfire being lit.
I can see the countryside.
I can feel gravel on the ground.
I can smell my lunch and the other horse's lunch being made.
I can feel the shavings on my hooves in my stable.
I can see all of the horses around me.
I always look forward to being ridden.
I can see cars when I am riding on the roads
And the smell of their exhaust fumes.

Hayley Holland (10)
Sibford Junior School, Banbury

Young Writers Information

We hope you have enjoyed reading this book - and that you will continue to enjoy it in the coming years.
If you like reading and writing poetry drop us a line, or give us a call, and we'll send you a free information pack.
Alternatively if you would like to order further copies of this book or any of our other titles, then please give us a call or log onto our website at www.youngwriters.co.uk

Young Writers Information
Remus House
Coltsfoot Drive
Peterborough
PE2 9JX
(01733) 890066